Reductions without Regret: Details

Avoiding Box Canyons, Roach Motels, and Wrong Turns

John A. Swegle and Douglas J. Tincher

Savannah River National Laboratory

The United States is concurrently pursuing the goals of reducing the size of its nuclear weapons force – strategic and non-strategic, deployed and non-deployed – and of modernizing the weapons it continues to possess. Many of the existing systems were deployed 30 to 50 years ago, and the modernization process can be expected to extend over the next decade or more. Given the impossibility of predicting the future over the lifetime of systems that could extend to the end of this century, it is essential that dead ends in force development be avoided, and the flexibility and availability of options be retained that allow for

- *Scalability downward in the event that further reductions are agreed upon;*
- *Reposturing to respond to changes in threat levels and to new nuclear actors; and*
- *Breakout response in the event that a competitor significantly increases its force size or force capability,*

In this paper, we examine the current motivations for reductions and modernization; review a number of historical systems and the attendant capabilities that have been eliminated in recent decades; discuss the current path forward for the U.S. nuclear force; provide a view of the evolving deterrence situation and our assessment of the uncertainties involved; and present examples of possibly problematic directions in force development. We close with our thoughts on how to maintain flexibility and the availability of options for which a need might recur in the future.

Introduction

Three factors are now shaping the evolution of the U.S. nuclear force: (1) the pursuit of nuclear-weapon reductions below current levels for all weapon types – strategic and non-strategic, deployed and non-deployed;[1,2] (2) modernization of a nuclear force developed during the Cold War and shaped by Cold-War politics and post-Cold-War expectations; and (3) diversification of nuclear deterrence from the bilateral Cold War standoff to a bi-level global-regional model. This third factor was implicitly acknowledged in the 2010 *Nuclear Posture Review Report*,[3] which numbers among its objectives

- Maintaining strategic deterrence and stability, and
- Strengthening regional deterrence and the assurance of our allies and partners.

The process of modernizing while reducing, in the face of a diversifying threat, is further complicated by the expected lifetimes of replacement systems, which can reasonably be expected to serve into the next century if necessary. Under the circumstances, it is essential that, to the maximum extent possible, flexibility be preserved, allowing both for *scalability downward* as the force size is reduced, the more likely course of action under current circumstances, or for *breakout responsiveness* if necessary, should circumstances change significantly for the worse – or perhaps the different – in the future.

In facing the dual processes of modernization and force reductions, a particular concern is that "box canyons," "roach motels," and "wrong turns" be avoided (see the text box for definitions). Each is problematic, with differing degrees of reversibility. In this paper, we consider the possibilities for losing, or compromising, key capabilities of the U.S. nuclear force in the face of modernization and reductions. To do so, we first review the stated goals for reduction, driving forces, and long-term goals. Second, we adopt an historical perspective, considering capabilities that were eliminated in past force reductions. Third, we attempt to define the needed capabilities looking forward in the context of the current framework for force modernization and the current picture of the evolving challenges of deterrence and assurance. Finally, we provide some suggested options for evaluating course corrections in force development in the event that the future turns out in unexpected ways.

Definitions

Roach Motels of Reduction: Dead ends in force development that are irreversible due to certain combinations of factors.

Box Canyons in the Valley of Disarmament: Courses of action resulting in undesirable force compositions or structures that can be reversed, albeit at the expense of "going back the way one came in."

Wrong Turns on the Road to the Future: Courses of action creating undesirable force compositions or structures that can be undone by a change of direction.

Goals for Reduction

The 2010 *Nuclear Posture Review Report*[4] frames the tension between reductions, stability, and deterrence in its five key objectives:

1. *Preventing nuclear proliferation and nuclear terrorism;*
2. *Reducing the role of U.S. nuclear weapons in U.S. national security strategy;*
3. *Maintaining strategic deterrence and stability at reduced nuclear force levels;*
4. *Strengthening regional deterrence and reassuring U.S. allies and partners; and*
5. *Sustaining a safe, secure, and effective nuclear arsenal.*

Overall, the current U.S. formulation aims to reduce all nuclear weapons, *strategic* and *non-strategic, deployed* and *non-deployed*. In this regard, strategic and non-strategic nuclear weapons are defined in terms of *range* (under the Intermediate-Range Nuclear Forces, or INF, Treaty, as well as New START, strategic nuclear missiles have ranges greater than 5,500 kilometers and thus global effect, while non-strategic weapons have shorter range and regional or theater effect); *delivery systems* (Strategic Nuclear Forces vs General Purpose or Tactical Dual-Capable Forces); and *release authority* (a national command authority *directs* the use of strategic nuclear weapons, but *authorizes* use of non-strategic nuclear weapons by a field commander). The distinction between deployed and non-deployed nuclear weapons was introduced in Article I of the Moscow Treaty (or SORT, for the Strategic Offensive Reductions Treaty), as "reentry vehicles on ICBMs in their launchers, reentry vehicles on SLBMs in their launchers onboard submarines, and nuclear armaments loaded on heavy bombers or stored in weapons storage areas of heavy bomber bases."[5] New START modified this definition by not separately counting nuclear armaments for bombers.

To put these definitions in perspective, on 3 May 2010, the U.S. Department of Defense publicly released a total number of 5,113 nuclear weapons in the U.S. stockpile.[6] This count included operationally-deployed warheads, those ready to be deployed, and inactive warheads maintained stored with their tritium bottles removed. In comparison, on 3 April 2013, the U.S. State Department released a Fact Sheet stating that the number of deployed nuclear weapons according to New START rules (notably counting heavy bombers but not their armaments) was 1,654.[7]

While the START series and the Moscow Treaty have regulated strategic nuclear weapons, the treatment of non-strategic nuclear weapons has been less comprehensive: the INF Treaty eliminated a class of non-strategic nuclear weapons for the Soviet Union (now Russia) and the United States, and the unilateral, non-binding Presidential Nuclear Initiatives (PNIs) of 1991 and 1992 by Presidents George H. W. Bush, Mikhail Gorbachev, and Boris Yeltsin represented an only partially successful attempt to regulate non-strategic nuclear weapons.[8]

On the U.S. side, the motivations for nuclear arms reductions are shifting from bilateral arms control to bilateral *plus* multilateral considerations related to: nonproliferation in the context of the nonproliferation regime, counterterrorism in the context of nuclear-arms security, and nuclear disarmament in the context of the long-term goal of eliminating nuclear weapons. Therefore, the dual desires of the U.S. to

- Regulate and limit non-strategic nuclear weapons, and
- Shift the motivation from bilateral arms control to multilateral reductions in pursuit of nonproliferation- and counterterrorism-oriented objectives that include eventual nuclear disarmament,

seem to indicate a need for enhanced flexibility in two major areas. First, it requires the ability to execute both global ("strategic") and regional ("tactical" or "non-strategic") missions with an integrated force subject to regulation by treaty or agreement across the force. Indeed, if a comprehensive arms control agreement is desired, these future regulations could extend beyond the deployed nuclear force to include conventional strategic forces, missile defense, non-deployed warheads and launchers, and the production infrastructure. Second, in the absence of the achievement of a broader agreement covering the NPT P-5 (the United States, Russia, China, France, and the United Kingdom), it requires a future nuclear force at presumably reduced size that retains flexibility allowing:

- Scalability downward in the event that further reductions are agreed upon, which defines a number of requirements, such as redundancy to guard against single-point failures, protection of viable career paths for the military personnel involved in the nuclear force, and provision of manageable "step sizes" for reduction;
- Reposturing to respond to changes in threat levels and to new nuclear actors, to allow for clear strategic messaging, and to reach a variety of targets even if additional forces are not needed; and
- Breakout response in the event that an adversary significantly increases its force size or force capability, which could involve upload capability, the ability to move non-deployed warheads or launchers back into the force, and the necessary production infrastructure, both built and latent. Potentially, breakout response could include the addition, or resurrection, of capabilities not resident in the current force.

Historical Perspectives

Before we address the future, we consider a number of previously eliminated nuclear-weapon systems, non-strategic and strategic, and the capabilities they represented. Specifically, we consider the Pershing II and Gryphon Ground-Launched Cruise Missile (GLCM); the Short-Range Attack Missile (SRAM); the nuclear-armed version of the Tomahawk Land-Attack Cruise Missile (TLAM/N); the Small ICBM (SICBM)/Midgetman; and the Peacekeeper/MX ICBM.

Pershing II and the GLCM were eliminated under the terms of the INF Treaty, as we shall discuss. Peacekeeper ultimately served out its lifetime as something of a failed bargaining chip in an attempt to secure the elimination of the Soviet Union's and Russia's heavy MIRVed missiles, as we shall discuss also. The other systems were all strongly affected by President George H.W. Bush's voluntary reduction and elimination measures of 1991 and 1992:[9]

- The reductions in the Presidential Address of 27 September 1991,[10] matched qualitatively by Presidents Gorbachev and Yeltsin, with the following features for the United States:
    - Short-range ground-launched weapon systems were eliminated, but air-delivered capabilities were retained;
    - Tactical naval nuclear weapons, including weapons delivered by carrier-based aircraft, were removed from normal deployment, with some eliminated and the rest moved to storage;
    - Rail-mobile and road-mobile ICBM development was terminated; and
    - SRAM II and SRAM T development was cancelled.
- President Bush's announcement, in his 1992 State of the Union message,[11] of the following:
    - Limitation of the B-2 bomber fleet to 20 aircraft, from the originally-planned 132;
    - Cancellation of Midgetman; and
    - Halting further production of the W88 SLBM warhead, the Peacekeeper ICBM, and the Advanced ALCM.

The unilateral, non-binding cuts in the Presidential Nuclear Initiatives (PNIs) of 1991 and 1992 were an attempt by both sides to reduce tensions, as well as the budget demands of nuclear weapons development, in the hopeful aftermath of the Cold War, although they were ultimately only partially effective on the Russian side.

Pershing II and the Ground-Launched Cruise Missile (GLCM)

Pershing II, armed with the W85 nuclear warhead, and the GLCM, armed with the W84, were highly-accurate (the former employing a maneuvering reentry vehicle, or MaRV), theater-based missiles with ranges of 1,770 and 2,500 kilometers, respectively. Both were eliminated entirely in 1988 under the terms of the INF Treaty in return for Soviet Union's total elimination of the SS-20 and SS-23, as well as the older SS-4 and SS-5 intermediate-range ballistic missiles (IRBMs).[*] That outcome was the result of an act of nuclear brinksmanship (see **Figure** 1), in which NATO voted in late 1979 to deploy Pershing II and the GLCM in Europe as part of a dual-track plan to counter the

---

[*] We note that the INF captures what is defined there as "shorter-range" (500-1,000 km), as well as medium- (1,000-3,500 km), and intermediate-range (3,500-5,500 km) ballistic and cruise missiles. Here we refer to all of these ranges as "INF-range."

Figure 1. Magazine cover from 31-Jan-1983.

3-warhead, 5,000-kilometer-range SS-20 while simultaneously calling for arms-control negotiations to reduce the numbers of these missiles to the lowest possible levels. The high accuracy and short flight times of the INF-range missiles between the Soviet Union and NATO countries created a serious First-Strike Stability issue for the two sides, and the Pershing II deployments in Europe generated an enormous controversy in NATO countries.

The politics of deploying and eliminating INF-range missiles illustrates the complexity and subtlety of Cold-War calculations. According to a summary[12] of the declassified version of a State Department cable describing the 1979 final report from the NATO High Level Group on the Pershing II and GLCM deployments, this move was meant to signal "Alliance resolve" and visibly fill any gaps in the escalation spectrum. According to Richard Garthoff, the warhead count on NATO INF-range missiles was kept at a lower level that of the Soviet side to signal that escalation to U.S. strategic systems was still possible and that isolation of a nuclear conflict to Europe was unlikely.[13] To demonstrate NATO-wide support, GLCMs were based not only in Germany, but also in Belgium, the Netherlands, and Italy. Further, to prevent the driving of wedges in the Alliance, the United States insisted that treaty negotiations be bipolar; Germany's coincident elimination of its Pershing IA missiles, which were to be armed with U.S. nuclear warheads, was formally a unilateral move.[14] Ultimately, the "zero option" of total elimination met with approval in Japan, where Prime Minister Yasuhiro Nakasone had been lobbying against any shift of such missiles to the east of the Ural Mountains.[15]

Short-Range Attack Missile (SRAM)

The SRAM A (AGM-69A, armed with the W69) was deployed between 1972 and 1975 for delivery by the B-52 and FB-111.[16] The initial purpose of these supersonic missiles was to strike air-defense targets to aid bombers in penetrating enemy air space; later, they were also intended to strike selected strategic targets. This original version was finally retired in 1990 because of motor reliability and warhead safety issues.

Two attempts were made to modernize and upgrade the original SRAM. Development of the SRAM B (AGM-69B) with a new motor to address motor storability problems and a new warhead to meet modern nuclear safety requirements, the W80, began in the late 1970s,[17] but was cancelled in 1978. When the B-1B bomber program was restarted in 1981, development began on a new SRAM II (AGM-131A, to be armed with the W89) for the bomber.[18] In addition, a modification, the SRAM T (AGM-131B, armed with the W91) was to be developed for delivery by the F-15E *Strike Eagle* dual-role fighter. A lighter, simpler, longer-lived, and more reliable rocket motor was designed to increase SRAM T range.

Unfortunately, as recounted in GAO reporting from 1991-1992,[19] problems with maneuverability and range (the latter tracing to issues with the propellant) were compromising the ability of SRAM II to meet the requirements to strike hardened targets from beyond enemy defenses and thus enhance bomber survivability. By the time President George H.W. Bush announced the cancellation of the

	SRAM II	ALCM	B61
Top Speed	Mach 2+	High subsonic	--
Range (km)	400	2,400+	--
Length (m)	3.18	6.3	3.56
Diameter (m)	0.39	0.62	0.33
Mass (kg)	900	1,430	320

Table 1. Comparison of the SRAM II, ALCM, and B61 gravity bomb.

programs in 1991, the range of SRAM II had been reduced to about that of SRAM A, and both SRAM II and SRAM T were years behind schedule at double the originally projected program costs. Cancellation of SRAM II and SRAM T left the U.S. with long-range, subsonic air-launched cruise missiles for delivery by strategic bombers, and B61 gravity bombs (see **Table 1**) for delivery by U.S. and NATO tactical dual-capable aircraft (T-DCA).

Tomahawk Land-Attack Cruise Missile/Nuclear (TLAM/N)

TLAM/N (BGM-109A), armed with the W80 nuclear warhead, provided medium-range (2,500 kilometers), tactical-nuclear delivery from a sea-based platform that did not require foreign nuclear basing. First deployed in the 1970s and carried by *Los Angeles*-class submarines, they were guided by a combination of inertial guidance and terrain contour matching (TERCOM).[†]

At-sea basing of TLAM/N was curtailed by the PNIs of 1991 and 1992, under which TLAM/N was removed from ships and submarines and placed in central storage on shore "under normal circumstances." This created the logistical challenge of having to return to port, or of developing alternate transport procedures to another location, to reload them onto submarines if desired. This would also have created a situation that restricted U.S. flexibility, in that redeploying TLAM/N under a situation of enhanced tensions would, if revealed, further raise tensions, whether that strategic signal was intended to be sent or not.

In addition to these logistical and flexibility issues, reliability had become a concern with TLAM/N

Figure 2. A crashed TLAM in a Turkish field, 29 March 2003.

based on the experience with conventionally-armed TLAM. In a 12 April 2003 press conference,[20] Adm. Timothy Keating, the commander of all maritime forces for the Operation Iraqi Freedom, indicated that "less than ten" of over 800 conventionally-armed TLAMs launched – "1 to 1.25 percent" – had failed to reach their targets and were found in Turkey or Saudi Arabia (see **Figure 2**[21]). This of course raised the specter of a loss-of-warhead scenario if a TLAM/N were to crash without properly destroying itself, in which case a number of possible scenarios presented themselves, depending on

---

[†] Different or upgraded guidance systems were employed on subsequent versions of conventionally-armed TLAM: the Tactical Anti-Ship Missile (TASM), and TLAM-C, -D, and -E.

whether the weapon crashed over friendly or unfriendly territory; whether it was recovered by a nuclear-armed or non-nuclear state, or a non-state actor; and whether the very difficult task of accessing the warhead intact could be accomplished in the face of the weapon's security features

Even so, TLAM/N was a tangible signal of extended deterrence, particularly in Northeast Asia. The April 2009 *Final Report of the Congressional Commission on the Strategic Posture of the U.S.*[22] highlighted the concerns of Asian allies regarding TLAM/N retirement, and a subsequent clarifying letter of December 2009 from Japan's Foreign Minister to Secretary of State Clinton, while expressing support for nuclear disarmament, requested continued clarification of the effect of retirement on extended deterrence for Japan.[23] These highlighted two features of extended deterrence in Northeast Asia. First, it showed the dependence of Japanese reception of U.S. extended deterrence on the political climate there: the Japanese election of 20 August 2009 featured a change in parties from the Liberal Democratic Party (under which comments were made to the Congressional Commission) to the Democratic Party of Japan (the party of the Foreign Minister writing the December letter). Second, it showed the importance of extended deterrence for Japan's national security, whatever the accepted means of providing it.

In the face of the aforementioned challenges, and others including the costs of modernizing TLAM/N, and in consideration of the ability to supplant this deterrent with other existing systems, and finally to meet the stated goal of reducing U.S. dependence on nuclear weapons, the elimination of TLAM/N was announced in the 2010 *Nuclear Posture Review Report.* Shortly thereafter, new nuclear deterrence consultations were established with both Japan and South Korea:

- Formation of an Extended Deterrence Policy Committee between the U.S. and the Republic of Korea was announced on 8 October 2010 in the Joint Communique of the U.S.-ROK Security Consultative Meeting in Washington, DC.[24]
- Establishment of an extended deterrence dialogue with Japan was announced in the joint statement issued at the conclusion of the 21 June 2011 U.S.-Japan Security Consultative Committee meeting.[25]

Presumably, in the rough equation for deterrence, *credibility = capability x commitment*, any reduction in capability with the retirement of TLAM/N is to be met, or exceeded, by the increased commitment shown to U.S. allies in Northeast Asia through the committee and dialogue.

Missile-X (MX) ICBM, "Peacekeeper"

From 1986 to 2005, Missile-X was the epitome of U.S. ICBM design and manufacture. Peacekeeper's advanced technologies modernized and improved U.S. nuclear deterrence and provided substantially-upgraded capacity:[26]

- Peacekeeper was the first U.S. ICBM to use "cold launch" technology, with steam pressure ejecting the missile from its silo to 150 feet above the silo doors, where first-stage ignition occurred;
- The missile used Kevlar fiber-reinforced composite construction for its solid-propellant rocket motor cases, which reduced structural mass versus traditional metal construction;
- It incorporated telescoping exit cones on its solid-fuel rocket engines to reduce missile length within the silo while retaining the performance of a longer missile in flight; and
- Its advanced solid propellants further boosted its payload throw weight, while its advanced micro-electronic guidance technologies enhanced accuracy.

Originally conceived in 1971 by the Strategic Air Command as a new, largest-ever, U.S. ICBM to replace what was believed to be obsolete Minuteman technology, the matter of how to provide a survivable basing mode for Peacekeeper created a painful, years-long controversy spanning the Carter and Reagan administrations that dogged the missile to the end of its deployment.[27] The problem was that defense analysts judged that two of the new SS-18 warheads could destroy a ten-warhead silo-based Peacekeeper, creating a 5-to-1 disadvantage in the so-called "exchange ratio." This was regarded as the possible source of strategic instability.[28]

After repeated consideration of a range of options including movement between Multiple Protective Shelters (MPSs), or rail-mobile launchers, or the unproven "superhard silo," a number of which aroused strong opposition from governors and representatives in states slated to host Peacekeeper, President Reagan chose possibly the most vulnerable option: basing in existing Minuteman silos. According to Pomeroy, this was the fastest route to deployment as a means of leveraging Peacekeeper to force arms control negotiations that would reduce or eliminate corresponding Soviet systems.[29] In 1993, the United States and Russia signed START II dictating the elimination of all multiple-warhead ICBMs. Under the circumstances, continued maintenance of Peacekeeper as a single-warhead delivery system made no sense, and even though START II was never ratified, deactivation of Peacekeepers began in 2003 and was completed in 2005.[30]

Peacekeeper embodied several capabilities or options for the U.S. nuclear force:

- The ability to deliver more than three MIRVs, which is the theoretical capability for Minuteman III (LGM-30G);
- The ability to deliver any future weapon system physically larger or heavier than the capacity of the upgraded Minuteman III; retaining Peacekeeper could have enabled the delivery of large, heavy maneuverable reentry vehicles (MaRVs) or boost-glide vehicles (BGVs), albeit at the expense of the increased verification burden created by the upload capacity of such a large booster; and
- The potential ability to deliver a ballistic RV along a non-Great Circle route trajectory in order to support weapon delivery options that avoided the political and legal complications of overflying Russia or other nations.

Small ICBM "Midgetman" (SICBM)

The SICBM concept represented a highly-optimized means of delivering a single nuclear warhead to roughly 11,000-km range with accuracy rivaling the MX (indeed, it was designed to carry the same Mark-21/W87 warhead).[31] The basing schema of widely-dispersed, self-contained, road- and off-road-mobile launchers provided enhanced survivability versus silos.[32] SICBM achieved its first successful test flight in mid-1991. However, President George H.W. Bush cancelled the SICBM program in early 1992 as a result of reduced strategic tensions due to the end of the Cold War.[33] Shortly afterward, Russia cancelled development of its own single-warhead *Kuryer* mobile ICBM.

Cancellation of SICBM made political and economic sense. The political pressure to curtail what was already a controversial project was substantial. The ever-reduced number of SICBMs to be procured, coupled to evolving system requirements, led to highly-scrutinized per-unit price escalations. Besides, Peacekeeper was already under construction with recovery of R&D costs well underway, whereas the SICBM price comparisons included all of these up-front and recoverable costs, making the larger Peacekeeper appear to be substantially less expensive.

Ultimately, SICBM's mobile launch platform could have led to a far more survivable ICBM force, at less expense than maintaining readiness for all silos to retain the high number of candidate targets facing enemy forces. SICBM would have been a wholly-new system optimized for single-warhead ICBM delivery. Launch could have occurred from anywhere the launcher could drive or anywhere the launcher could be transported by rail, ship, or air.[34] Eventual negotiations for fewer warheads and missiles could theoretically be more acceptable as a result of the increased survivability of each remaining mobile missile versus fixed silos. Verification would be simpler in that SICBM was designed to only accommodate one RV. Finally, contingency replacement of existing, or breakout production of new, airframes would have been simpler if the production lines of the newer system had been retained and used for spares throughout the program's lifetime.

Pros and Cons of the Eliminated Nuclear Capabilities

In **Table 2**, we summarize the capabilities of the non-strategic nuclear weapon systems described here, the contributions they offered for nuclear deterrence (the pros), and the complications they presented for stability or nuclear security (the cons).

	Capability	Pro	Con
Pershing II	INF-range ballistic missile Maneuvering RV	Responsive theater ballistic missile Highly accurate	Strongly destabilizing Overseas nuclear weapon basing
GLCM	INF-range cruise missile	Responsive theater nuclear weapon Highly accurate	Strongly destabilizing Overseas nuclear weapon basing Subsonic, potential in-flight loss of weapon
SRAM II/T	100s kilometer range tactical standoff missile	Responsive tactical standoff weapon Supersonic Potentially highly accurate	Overseas nuclear weapon basing Potential in-flight loss of weapon (reduced chance) Possibly redundant with ALCM Program behind schedule and over budget when cancelled
TLAM/N	Sea-launched regional deterrent	Responsive theater nuclear weapon Highly accurate Can avoid overseas nuclear basing	Logistics of deployment under PNIs Subsonic, potential in-flight loss of weapon Launch temporarily locates submarine Needing modernization when eliminated
Table 2. Capabilities, pros, and cons of the eliminated non-strategic nuclear weapons discussed here.			

INF-range missiles were eliminated by the United States and the Soviet Union because of the strategic instability they created. Since then, though, confrontations involving MRBM- and IRBM-armed nations have developed – or are developing – in several key regions outside Europe:

- In the Middle East, Israel possesses Jericho-II (1,500 kilometers), and Iran is allegedly developing Sejil-2/3 (2,500-4,000 kilometers), Shahab-4 (2,000-4,000 kilometers), and BM-25 (2,500-4,000 kilometers);
- In South Asia, India has deployed Agni-II (2,000-3,000 kilometers), and Agni-IV (3,000-3,500 kilometers), and has others in the R&D phase, and Pakistan has Ghauri-III and the Shaheen-3+ series all in the R&D phase; and

- In Northeast Asia, North Korea is developing IRBMs (Musudan/BM-25, as well as Unha-3 and KN-08, the range of which could extend into ICBM territory), and China possesses DF-4 (4,500-5,000 km) and DF-21 (2,150 km) and has others under development.

Even in the absence of the INF Treaty, an examination of sample ranges between example basing points in the three regions – Aviano Air Base in Italy for the Middle East, British territory at Diego Garcia for the Indian Ocean region, and Anderson Air Force Base on Guam for the Western Pacific – shows that ranges to points in the Middle East, South Asia, and the Western Pacific all exceed the range of Pershing II, requiring a more muscular missile closer in performance to the SS-20 or Midgetman (see **Table 3**). We note that of course basing at Aviano would only reprise the tense

From Guam to:	Distance (km)	From Diego Garcia to:	Distance (km)	From Aviano AB to:	Distance (km)
Beijing	4,000	Abu Dhabi	3,900	Abu Dhabi	4,400
Hanoi	4,200	Bandar Abbas	4,100	Bandar Abbas	4,400
Manila	2,550	Colombo	4,000	Cairo	2,400
Pyongyang	3,400	Islamabad	4,400	Damascus	2,400
Quanzhou	3,000	Karachi	3,500	Kiev	1,400
Seoul	3,200	Kolkota	3,700	Minsk	1,400
Shanghai	3,100	Muscat	3,600	Moscow	2,100
Shenzen	3,400	New Delhi	4,000	Riyadh	3,800
Singapore	4,700	Riyadh	4,500	St. Petersburg	1,900
Tokyo	2,500	Singapore	3,600	Tehran	3,400
Yangon	5,200	Tehran	5,200	Tel Aviv	2,400

Table 3. Distances between example points for a hypothetical consideration of medium- and intermediate-range missile basing.

and unstable Cold War situation that created a need on both sides for the INF Treaty, and which would likely be politically untenable in all but the most difficult-to-envision circumstances. Basing options in the Middle East or Northeast Asia that would shorten the distances there, possibly even involving deployment of mobile missiles with their transporter-erector launchers from the U.S. using C-17s, could be imagined, but the political-military issues involved are substantial, complex, and beyond the scope of this paper. Clearly, submarine basing of a conventionally-armed missile, or use of SLBMs or ALCMs, would have to be evaluated as alternatives.

Context is significant for the elimination of SRAM and TLAM/N. At the time of their elimination, both would have required significant further expenditures to either reach or continue deployment: SRAM was years behind schedule, well over budget, and slipping in promised performance. TLAM/N was limited by the pledge that it would normally be kept on-shore in central storage, which raised the issue that its deployment to sea would likely be not only a response to a crisis, but also a very strong signal that could raise tensions even further. Further, in-flight failures of conventionally-armed TLAMs, although limited in number, posed the prospect of a low-probability/high-consequence loss-of-weapon event for TLAM/N. In this context, elimination of SRAM and TLAM/N, were interpretable as the result of a confluence of programmatic opportunism in cancelling troubled programs and strategic optimism at the end of the Cold War or in the context of reducing the role of nuclear weapons in U.S. security strategy.

Table 4 summarizes the pros and cons of the eliminated strategic nuclear weapons.

	Capability	Pro	Con
Peacekeeper	Heavy lift Heavily MIRVed High-energy booster	Highly accurate Surviving missiles highly destructive even in small numbers Economies of scale at large force sizes	Silo basing vulnerable, creating a highly attractive target Mobile basing in Multiple Protected Shelters highly unpopular Superhard silos not fully explored Upload capacity creates verification challenge
Midgetman	Road-mobile Optimized single-warhead missile	Accuracy approaching that of silo-based systems Survivable land-based option Single warhead simplifies verification	Additional cost created by need to build stand-alone system that doesn't capitalize on existing silos Mobile basing potentially problematic with hosting states

Table 4. Capabilities, pros, and cons of the eliminated strategic nuclear weapon systems discussed here.

As recounted by Pomeroy, the missile concept that evolved into Peacekeeper was always based on the assumption that the missile would have some sort of mobile or relocatable basing scheme to increase its survivability. Based in existing Minuteman silos, Hobson showed that Peacekeeper suffered a highly disadvantageous 5-to-1 loss ratio to a pair of incoming warheads. This is potentially the source of a so-called First-Strike Instability[35] in which the U.S. leadership might have felt a "use or lose" imperative to launch preemptively, or on warning of attack, in order to prevent the loss of the substantial part of its nuclear force tied up in vulnerable Peacekeeper warheads. Midgetman, on the other hand, with its dispersed force of single-warhead missiles, was not the source of such a strategic instability. And the instability situation was not so clear-cut: submarine-based missiles (for which accuracy was improving with the transition from Polaris to Trident) and the possible addition of Midgetman to the force, provided a survivable, and therefore at least partially, stabilizing backup. Nevertheless, the potential instability associated with heavily-MIRVed missiles was a driving force in the negotiation in START II, which provided for the complete elimination of ICBMs carrying more than one warhead.

START II never entered into force. Russia continues to deploy MIRVed missiles, silo-based and road-mobile, along with mobile, single-warhead ICBMs and submarine-based missiles that strengthen strategic stability. Beyond the issue of stability, consider two other perspectives:

- Multiple-warhead ICBMs can be used to change the offense-defense dynamics in the face of U.S. ballistic missile defense by making it easier to synchronize the launch of a larger number of warheads in order to overpower the defense, since fewer missiles are required for the same number of warheads.

- The relative numbers of MIRVed and single-warhead ICBMs can influence expected escalation dynamics. If one faces an adversary with heavily-MIRVed, silo-based missiles, the putative attacker is presumably put in a position of attempting to take them all or accept the heavy consequences of retaliation by any surviving missiles. In this sense, the deployment of heavily-MIRVed missiles can "steepen the escalation ladder," creating a heavy burden on the potential attacker to be able to mount a very large initial attack. This steepening of the escalation ladder both raises the bar for first use, but potentially increases the planned size of an initial exchange.

Defining the Needed Capabilities

Figure 3 outlines the current U.S. nuclear force:

- Minuteman III carrying either the W78 in the Mk-12A RV or the W87 in the Mk-21 RV;
- Trident D5 on the *Ohio*-class SSBN carrying either the W76 in the Mk-4 RV or the W88 in the Mk-5 RV;
- The Air-Launched Cruise Missile (ALCM, AGM-86B) carrying the W80 warhead, which is currently delivered by the B-52H bomber;
- The B83 gravity bomb, which can be delivered by the B-52H and B-2 bombers; and
- The B61 gravity bomb, delivered by the B-52H and B-2 heavy bombers, as well as the F-16, F-15E, [‡] and Tornado T-DCA; in the future, the F-35 is expected to take on the tactical delivery role.

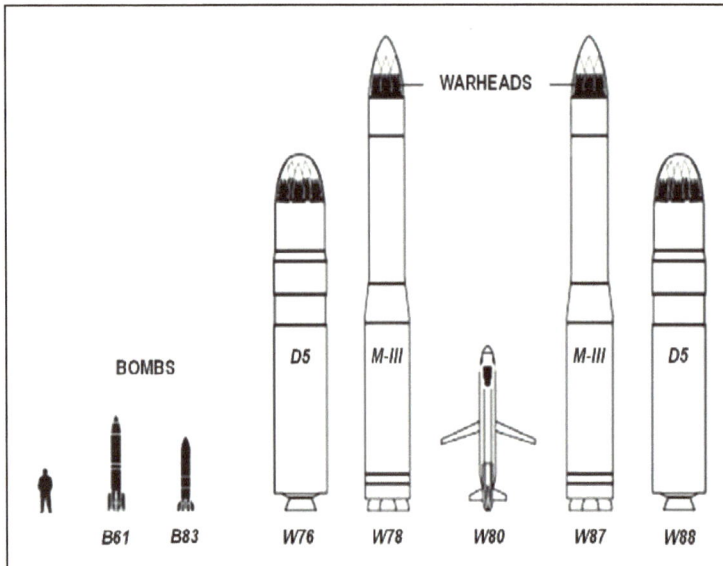

Figure 3. The current nuclear force, showing the Minuteman III ICBM (MM-III) and Trident D5 SLBM.

According to 2011 reporting from the General Accounting Office,[36] the former GLCM warhead, the W84, remains in "managed retirement" status. With a modern design, the W84 is available for use if required.

The U.S. is in the process of modernizing the nuclear force, with a program that currently preserves the same basic force structure. As shown in **Table 5**, there are programs underway to replace the ALCM; the heavy bombers; the *Ohio*-class SSBN; and the Minuteman III ICBM.

[‡] The long-term fate of the F-15E as a B-61 delivery system remains uncertain. The F-35 is claimed by the USAF as a replacement for the F-16; F-35 is not stated as a replacement for the F-15E. Apparently, if the AFRL's Adaptive Engine Technology Development program is fully successful, the USAF will need to consider wholesale replacement of its current F-15E fleet with: new-manufacture F-15Es; a wholesale redesign of a two-seat, long-endurance variant of the F-35; or placing this mission in the LRS-B box.

System	Enter Service	Service Life	Replacement
B-52H	1961-62	~2040	Long Range Strike-Bomber (LRS-B)
ALCM	1982-	~2030	Long-Range Standoff (LRSO)
W80	1982	--	Life extension or replacement with existing warhead*
B61	1979-97	~2050	Life extension
B83	1983	--	To be determined
B-2 (B61, B83, *LRSO*)	1994-2000	~2060	Long Range Strike-Bomber (LRS-B)
Minuteman III	1970-78	2030	To be determined
W78	1979		Life extension
W87	1986		Life extension
Ohio-class SSBN	1976-97	2031	*Ohio* Replacement Submarine
Trident II (D5)	1990	2042	Life extension
W76	1978		Life extension
W88	1989		Life extension
Tactical air, F-16 (B61)	1981	~2020	F-35
Tactical air, F-15E (B61)	1986	~2030	To be determined
Table 5. Modernization plan for the U.S. nuclear force.			*pending approval*

According to reporting of an April 2013 talk by Air Force Secretary Michael Donley, the next strategic bomber is being developed under the Long Range Strike-Bomber (LRS-B) program, with the goal of producing 80-100 bombers that will become operational in the mid-2020s.[37] Although the bomber is expected to be manned originally, to date a capability for operating LRS-B unmanned is included in the program plan.

Department of Defense budgeting documents for fiscal year 2013 show that Long-Range Standoff (LRSO), the program to develop a successor to the ALCM, is proceeding with completion of the Analysis of Alternatives, a stage in the overall acquisition process. The same documents indicate that the Technology Development effort is to begin in 2015, with planned completion of that phase in 2017.[38] Current planning is for the B-2 to carry the LRSO as well.[39]

A January 2013 Broad Agency Announcement (BAA) entitled "Ground Based Strategic Deterrence" solicited the preparation of white papers for "concepts that address modernization or replacement of the ground based leg of the nuclear triad."[40] Beyond a baseline concept to retain the current Minuteman III system to 2075 with no plan to close capability gaps, the BAA outlines four additional concepts that are to be explored in the solicited white paper:

- Current Fixed Concept – Retaining the fixed-basing mode, modernize the Minuteman III "in the sub-component areas of guidance, propulsion, reentry vehicles/reentry systems, nuclear command, control and communications (NC3) and ground infrastructure."
- New Fixed Concept – Develop a new, super-hard silo, and a new missile.

- Mobile Concept – Develop a new transporter erector launcher (TEL) for on- or off-road operation to carry and launch a new missile. The white paper is to consider the possibility that the missile could carry up to two Mk-12A or Mk-21 reentry vehicles.
- Tunnel Concept – Based in a subway-like tunnel with openings at regular intervals, a single new missile is to be carried on an unmanned transporter/launcher.

In all four cases, the white papers are to evaluate the MIRV capability of the missile, while the last three also require the evaluation of the adaptability of the missile to deliver Trajectory Shaping Vehicles / Trajectory Correcting Vehicles (TSV/TCV) for the reentry vehicle(s).

The progress of the *Ohio* replacement, or SSBN(X), program was described in a March 2013 report from the Congressional Research Service.[41] This report states that the Navy intends to build 12 of the new SSBNs, in order to have 10 available at all times, since at any time, two are planned to be undergoing lengthy maintenance. Each submarine is planned to have 16 launch tubes, as opposed to the 20 active launch tubes currently available (of 24 originally installed) on *Ohio*-class SSBNs. The submarines are expected to have a 40-year lifetime, with no refueling of the nuclear reactors during that span. Roughly the same size as the current SSBNs, SSBN(X) will have quieter all-electric propulsion. Procurement of the first boat has been pushed back two years to 2021, the result of which will be that during the period 2029-2041, only 10 or 11 boats will be available, although the Navy states that none will be in maintenance during that period, so that the ten-boat criterion will be met.

The *Fiscal Year 2014 Stockpile Stewardship and Management Plan* for the Department of Energy outlines the directions for the life extension of existing warheads and a restructuring of the mix of nuclear explosives to be carried by the nuclear force.[42] This restructuring would change the warhead assignments shown in Table 5, to varying degrees depending on the future implementation of the plan. Current directions from the Nuclear Weapons Council include life extension of the B61 (the Mod 12 version), completion of production of the W76-1, completion of the next phase of modernization of the W78/88-1, and downward adjustment of the mix of active and reserve status for the B83.

In the longer term, the Weapons Council has endorsed a "3+2" vision for U.S. nuclear explosive systems that involves 3 missile-deliverable nuclear-explosive systems and 2 air-delivered systems; the intent is for each weapon type – missile- or air-deliverable – to be *interoperable*[§] across the delivery systems for its respective type (i.e., either ICBMs and SLBMs or cruise missiles and bombs). The first missile-deliverable Interoperable Warhead (IW-1) is to be a life-extended version of the W78/88-1. At this time, two additional such warheads, IW-2 and IW-3, have not been specifically determined, but the expectation is that they will be based on the W87/88 and W76-1.

Looking Forward: The Nuclear Deterrence Missions

Returning to the 2010 *Nuclear Posture Review Report*, we see that in a context in which the United States aims to reduce the role of nuclear weapons in U.S. national security strategy, the two major deterrence goals are to:

[§] Interoperable warheads are defined in the 2014 Stockpile Stewardship plan as "warheads with a common [nuclear explosive package] integrated with non-nuclear systems that maximize the use of common and adaptable components," which are meant to be deployable on multiple delivery platforms.

- Maintain <u>strategic deterrence and stability</u> at a reduced nuclear force level, condensing weapon variants and types, while reducing total numbers; eliminating weapons or weapon types if possible; and maximizing latent capability to replace critical systems; and
- Strengthen <u>regional deterrence and reassure</u> U.S. Allies and partners, shoring up posture and doctrinal statements ensuring confidence in U.S. deterrence.

For the foreseeable future, we anticipate that the nuclear deterrence mission will have global and regional aspects, as depicted in **Figure 4**.

- The five NPT Nuclear-Weapon States, shown in black in the figure, all have nuclear weapons with global reach.
- The NATO nations (in blue) reaffirmed in the 2010 Strategic Concept that NATO is a nuclear alliance.[43]
- The nations of the Middle East (in red) include those nations between Egypt in the west and Iran to the east, and the involvement of NATO state Turkey is significant as well.
- South Asia (in yellow) primarily involves India and Pakistan, although China is a factor in that dynamic, also.
- In the Western Pacific (in green), the U.S. participates in nuclear deterrence consultative bodies with Japan and South Korea, and Australia's *2013 Defence White Paper* continues the Australian policy of embracing U.S. extended nuclear deterrence.[44] China, Russia, and North Korea are involved in the nuclear security dynamic of the Western Pacific. On the other hand, the nations of Southeast Asia are members of the *Southeast Asian Nuclear-Weapon-Free Zone* governed by the *Treaty of Bangkok*.

The nuclear capabilities of the declared nuclear nations are synopsized in **Table 6**. This table does not include Israel, which maintains official ambiguity about its nuclear status and does not discuss its delivery capabilities. Table 6 also does not include North Korea, which declares that it possesses

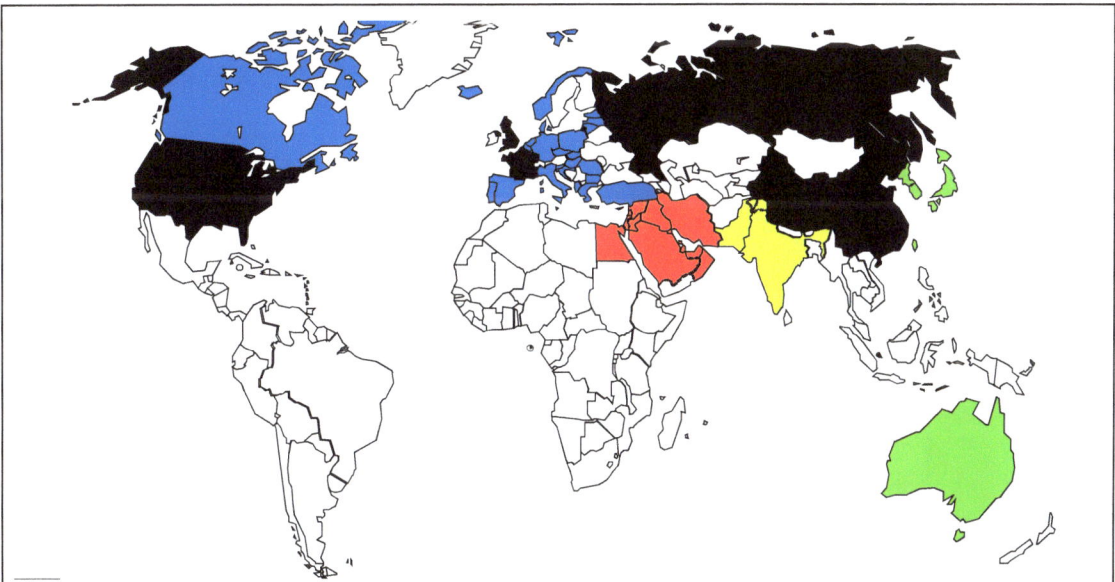

Figure 4. The five Nuclear-Weapon States defined by the Nuclear Nonproliferation Treaty (or P5, in black), and the four regions in which nuclear weapons play a significant role in regional security: the Euro-Atlantic region (blue, plus Russia, the United States, the UK, and France); the Middle East (red); South Asia (yellow, plus China); and the Western Pacific (green, plus Russia, the United States, and China.

	Land-Based Ballistic Missiles	Sub-Based Ballistic Missiles	Aircraft-Delivered
United States	ICBM	Intercontinental	T-DCA, Strategic
Russia	ICBM	Intercontinental	T-DCA, Strategic
China	MRBM, IRBM, ICBM	Medium-range, Intercontinental	--
France	--	Intercontinental	T-DCA
United Kingdom	--	Intercontinental	--
India	SRBM, MRBM, IRBM	Short-range	T-DCA
Pakistan	SRBM, MRBM, IRBM	--	T-DCA
Table 6. Delivery capabilities of the declared nuclear states			

the elements of a nuclear program, but has not demonstrated the integration of a nuclear weapon. In the absence of having apparently produced a nuclear weapon capability, Iran is also not on the table. Note that only the U.S. and Russia possess a full, intercontinental-range nuclear triad, although India is close to developing a regional nuclear triad with its soon-to-be-commissioned nuclear submarine and tests of an underwater-launched ballistic missile.

In view of the circumstances, we sketch out the following current and expected strategic and regional nuclear deterrence missions, bearing in mind that the projected lifetimes for the strategic systems under development will stretch well beyond the foreseeable future:

- U.S.-Russia strategic – With the two largest nuclear forces comprised of the large majority of all nuclear weapons – in part a consequence of history, in part a reflection of the U.S. role in the world and Russia's position spanning most of the northern part of the Eurasian land mass – this deterrence relationship provides much of the motivation for each nation's nuclear triad. Although highly regulated and symmetrized by arms control agreements at the strategic nuclear end, other elements of the relationship – non-strategic nuclear weapons, missile defense, non-nuclear strategic capability, conventional military capability– remain much more asymmetric.[45]

- NATO/Euro-Atlantic regional – With three nuclear-weapon states in the alliance, NATO reaffirmed its commitment to nuclear deterrence in the *2010 Strategic Concept*: "As long as nuclear weapons exist, NATO will remain a nuclear alliance." For NATO, this includes collective nuclear defense planning and the concept of *nuclear sharing*, in which some non-nuclear members of the alliance are prepared to deliver U.S. nuclear weapons in time of war. Beyond the presence of Russian nuclear weapons in the region, Iran remains a potential threat on the periphery.

- U.S.-China strategic – This constitutes a mission for the U.S. triad and China's ICBMs and nascent submarine-borne deterrent. A highly asymmetric relationship, China has far fewer nuclear weapons, but theater-specific capability not matched by the U.S. and a developing anti-access/area-denial capability potentially affecting U.S. effectiveness regionally.

- Western Pacific extended – The U.S. has extended-deterrence relationships with Japan and South Korea, as well as substantial numbers of troops stationed in each country. In addition, as mentioned previously, Australia relies on the extension of nuclear deterrence by the U.S., and is preparing to host 2,500 U.S. Marines in the country. China possesses regional nuclear missiles, and North Korea possesses the elements of a nuclear force, regardless of its current ability to deliver nuclear weapons.

- Middle East regional – The U.S. has a strong alliance relationship with Israel, and should an Iranian nuclear threat become a reality, the U.S. role in the region could shift from dissuasion to deterrence, perhaps involving more formal extended-deterrence relationships with nations in the region if the proper constellation of alliances can be developed.
- South Asia regional – Although the United States has strong nonproliferation and nuclear-security concerns in South Asia, it does not have the same military alliance relationships and attendant nuclear-deterrence involvement in that region that it does elsewhere. Moreover, there are elements of resentment of the United States by both Pakistan and India that are exacerbated by mistrust of each other.[46, 47, 48]

Observations on the Strategic Deterrence Mission

The United States has entered a period in which the nuclear-deterrence mission is complicated not only by the increasingly multilateral nature of the problem, and the growing regionalization, but by the fact that recapitalization of the U.S. nuclear force is growing in urgency. Against this backdrop, we offer three observations on the strategic deterrence mission.

First, in the coming years, the cost of *recapitalization* and of *maintenance and operation* of the enduring force will be a major consideration, perhaps *the* major consideration. The current U.S. nuclear triad was conceived, designed, and built during the Cold War or in its immediate aftermath. It was formed, and its size was determined, by the bilateral strategic competition between two irreconcilable political-economic-social systems. Decision making was clearer cut under the circumstances, although even so, military decisions about the deployment of INF-range missiles or enhanced-radiation nuclear warheads (the so-called "neutron bomb") were enormously controversial and the subject of election battles at the time for NATO allies.

For a variety of reasons, there has been a gap of some two to three decades in the development and deployment of new U.S. strategic nuclear systems. Other P5 states have moved past, or are moving through, this stage already:

- Although Russia was in a more precarious state when it was renegotiating the expiring START agreement, it has begun to move past that point, deploying new road-mobile missiles – with single or multiple warheads – commencing development of what could be a large liquid-fueled successor to the ten-warhead SS-18,[49] completing development and beginning deployment of two new SLBMs (*Liner* and *Bulava*), and building the submarines to carry them.
- China continues to build and develop new nuclear weapon systems. In recent years, it has deployed the road-mobile DF-31A, capable of reaching much of the U.S., it has built and continues to build a new SSBN (*Jin*-class), it is completing development of the SLBM for that submarine, and it is apparently developing a new, road-mobile, multiple-warhead ICBM.[50]
- France has four relatively new *Triomphant*-class SSBNs (commissioned between 1997 and 2010), it has developed a new nuclear warhead for its air-launched cruise missiles, and it will deploy a new nuclear warhead on the M51 SLBM currently under development and slated for deployment in 2015.[51]
- Although the U.K.'s nuclear deterrent force remains a subject of public debate, the 2006 document, *The Future of the United Kingdom's Nuclear Deterrent*, painted a clear picture: the current nuclear warhead would either be extended or replaced with a decision to be made in about 2025; the Trident D5 missile employed by the UK would be life extended,

with a decision about possible replacement made in about 2035; and the process of replacing the *Vanguard*-class SSBNs, commissioned between 1993 and 1999, would begin in about 2025.[52]

In this context, with increasing complexity in the mission space, faced with the substantial cost of recapitalization, and constrained by U.S. budget realities, two points jump to the fore:

- Indecision born of complexity, and conflicted motivations created by the desire to reduce forces and the reliance on nuclear weapons, must be avoided if the United States is to prevent a reprise of the MX/Peacekeeper situation. There, an expensive, multiyear process played out when an escalatory, albeit technically superior, weapon system was developed as a match for the SS-18; then held hostage to repeated reviews of the same basing options; then compromised by the unpopular politics of the most effective mobile basing modes; and ultimately deployed in a strategically undesirable basing mode largely as a bargaining chip to motivate Soviet reductions in heavily-MIRVed missiles (a move ultimately defeated by evolving circumstances).
- If indeed the costs of force recapitalization are onerous, to what extent will the United States be able to use arms control measures to mitigate the burden, negotiating Russia down to numbers or force structures deemed more manageable on the U.S. end? And to what value, economically and in a political-military sense? Lastly, what strategies are available, and what compromises will be required?

Second, one must ask if, or at what point as the force is reduced, the triad becomes unviable. To be certain, the numbers of warheads are a major issue. To restate the obvious, we must ask at what force size it becomes impossible to maintain the nuclear triad at something greater than "critical mass?" Alternatively, are there a number of warheads at which a sort of "phase change" occurs in the constitution of the force? Finally, is there a supportable mix of nuclear- and conventionally-armed strategic systems that mitigates the operational effects of nuclear reductions while satisfying the international political and strategic stability demands?

- Do unit costs, for construction, maintenance, and effective command and control rise to unjustifiable levels?
- With fewer, and smaller, units, do the military career paths become unattractive for our best officers? Will a combined strategic force of both nuclear- and conventionally-armed systems sustain those career paths?

Along a different line, the character of each element of the triad – ICBMs, SSBNs/SLBMs, and heavy bombers – depends essentially on the continued existence of the triad. Our understanding of that configuration was developed in the context of bilateral deterrence; however, in each of the three possible dyads, the role of each element changes in subtle ways. To return to an example we discussed earlier, the silo-based Peacekeeper, taken alone or perhaps as an element of a dyad with strategic bombers, created a strategic instability because of the unfavorable exchange rates for the defense (warheads lost to an attack versus the number of warheads required to attack successfully); however, the addition of survivable submarine-based missiles stabilized that situation.

The challenge of anticipating the issues in order to achieve an orderly reduction of the nuclear force raises two further questions:

- Is the United States prepared for the case in which it not only reduces strategic nuclear weapons, but in which it rolls strategic and non-strategic weapons together and places limits on the total?
- Viewing this last issue in a different way: What flexibility and scalability – downward, but if necessary, upward – are needed and do the available options provide? As an example, the 16-tube SSBN(X) represents smaller "steps" for force reduction than the 24-tube, or 20-tube, *Ohio*-class SSBN. Similarly, single-warhead ICBMs such as Midgetman scale downward more easily than heavily-MIRVed missiles, particularly as the numbers dwindle, but fail to provide upload capability for rapid upward scaling if that is required.

Third, we offer some specific thoughts for two elements of the triad. With regard to ICBMs, we note the following:

- The broader nuclear-deterrence role of ICBMs is clouded by the problem that purely ballistic missiles and RVs must overfly Russia to reach almost all targets of current interest. This complicates the deterrence challenge. As Schelling has pointed out,[53] "Deterrence is concerned with the exploitation of potential force." The overflight issue raises a number of questions:
  - Does the overflight issue create a threshold for U.S. ICBM launch, below which overflight is not worth the trouble?
  - Will U.S. responses be delayed by a more complex decision-making process, and perhaps the need to warn Russia of impending overflight, or by the need to use SLBMs instead, which in many cases are slower to launch?
  - Would a future U.S. administration feel the need to seek permission, making Russia a participant in the decision-making process?

  These questions all increase the uncertainty of U.S. nuclear use and thus degrade U.S. deterrent capability. This, of course, raises the issues of whether maneuvering warheads (or trajectory-shaping or trajectory-correcting vehicles) could be used, or if perhaps boosters can be developed to fly non-minimum-energy trajectories in order to inject ballistic RVs into non-overflight trajectories. In either case, the challenge is to find the means by which the available non-overflight target set can be expanded. Otherwise, the United States will be faced with the issue of addressing the overflight of Russia to employ ICBMs in a deterrence role against potential targets in the Western Pacific and the Middle East.
- Have potential adversaries' advances in accuracy, for the yields available, made different basing modes than current silos necessary? Are there future scenarios in which mobile ICBMs would be necessary to assure survivability and strategic stability, particularly at lower numbers, and what features of those scenarios dictate mobility?
- Does the U.S. wish to retain some upload capability, even if only in maintaining a reserve margin in the throw weight of the boosters?
- Ultimately, beyond the rapid response that ICBMs can provide, ICBMs enhance deterrence by dispersing and increasing the nuclear target set presented to a U.S. adversary, a point made by Keith Payne in 2012 Congressional testimony.[54] Drawing on analysis by Johnson, Bowie, and Haffa,[55] Payne pointed out that eliminating ICBMs in favor of a nuclear dyad of SSBNs and B-2 bombers reduced the number of aim points to five (two submarine bases and three bomber bases) from five *plus* the number of missile silos (which is now 450).

With regard to SLBMs, the following points stand out:

- In launching SLBMs, SSBNs identify their location, at least for a time. Given the expected lifetimes for the next generation of SSBNs, this raises the question of whether planners must anticipate a future in which long-endurance armed drones are deployed to provide top-cover for submarine launches, or, alternatively, are deployed in an anti-submarine role to defend against SLBM launches.
- What are the arguments for and against two-ocean basing of SSBNs?
- Should the U.S. build 8, 10, or 12 *Ohio* replacement submarines, and should each have 16 or 20 launch tubes, as discussed by Woolf?[56]
- What is the associated scalability of our SSBN force downward under reductions and upward as a hedge?

Observations on the Challenges of Regional and Extended Deterrence

As the complexity of regional and extended deterrence grows, drawing in part from the 2010 *Nuclear Posture Review Report*, it appears that within the constraints of the current nuclear force, there are three elements to regional deterrence:

- Enhanced consultation with allies and partners;
- Regional deployment of heavy bombers and T-DCA; and
- Use of "strategic" systems in "tactical" roles.

NATO has a history of consultation in support of its nuclear-sharing arrangement, primarily through the *Nuclear Planning Group*.[57] In Northeast Asia, following the announcement of the elimination of TLAM/N, strengthened consultation was established with South Korea in late 2010 via the *U.S.-ROK Extended Deterrence Policy Committee*, and with Japan in 2011 via the *U.S.-Japan Extended Deterrence Dialogue*.

Regional deployment outside the U.S. and NATO is a serious challenge. The Presidential Nuclear Initiatives in 1991 and 1992 eliminated nuclear basing in South Korea, and made temporary regional basing of non-strategic nuclear weapons on aircraft carriers and attack submarines unlikely under peacetime conditions. Elimination of TLAM/N finally eliminated the sea-based nuclear cruise missile option, following earlier elimination of carrier basing.

In-theater basing of nuclear weapons in the Western Pacific is complicated by a number of factors:

- In Japan, repeatedly reaffirmed national policy has limited or prevented "introduction" of foreign nuclear weapons;
- Australia, although the beneficiary of extended nuclear deterrence, is a signatory of the *Treaty of Rarotonga* and a member of the *South Pacific Nuclear-Weapon-Free Zone*; and
- Although North Korea has arguably invalidated the treaty, South Korea is nevertheless a party to the *1992 Joint Declaration of South and North Korea on the Denuclearization of the Korean Peninsula*.

Guam, of course, is U.S. territory; however, as indicated in Table 3, ranges from Anderson Air Force Base to Northeast Asia are substantial. Regional deployment of heavy bombers is logistically complicated if an "air bridge" of refueling tankers must be established, although B-52s[58] and B-2s[59] recently provided a demonstration of U.S. extended deterrence capability in South Korea. Temporary basing in-theater would presumably require the existence of adequately safe and secure nuclear facilities at Anderson AFB.

The Middle East presents similar challenges. Referring back to Table 3, one can see that the British territory of Diego Garcia is at least as far from the Middle East as Guam is from Northeast Asia. The NATO airbase at Aviano, on the other hand, is much closer. More to the point, though, the U.S. still has not established the same extended deterrence relationships in that region that exist in the Euro-Atlantic and Western Pacific regions.

From a deterrence standpoint, given the lack of a U.S. non-strategic nuclear weapon other than T-DCA armed with B61 gravity bombs, and given the possession of more non-strategic nuclear options by Russia and China, one can reasonably ask whether the totality of U.S. nuclear-deterrence options are <u>credible</u>, <u>sufficient</u>, and <u>appropriate</u> to the regional missions of:

- Phase-0 deterrence;[60]
- Assurance, and reassurance, of allies and partners; and
- Escalation control, from crisis through to conflict.

Under current circumstances, U.S. deterrence and, if necessary, escalation control, will depend in large measure on the employment of "strategic" nuclear weapons in a "regional" role. We will return to this issue shortly, but here, we pose three questions about this "crossover" role for strategic nuclear weapons:

- Will the fog of war obscure the difference between "tactical" and "strategic?"
- Are there intrinsically different features for regional nuclear capabilities – distinguished by range, penetrability, yield, or numbers – that send a usefully different message? (see the following text box)
- If indeed there are usefully different features for regional nuclear capabilities – not a settled question – would this create a need for dual-capable strategic nuclear systems (e.g., a low-yield SLBM warhead) or a T-DCA-deliverable modification of LRSO?

Box Canyons, Roach Motels, and Wrong Turns

Table 7, discussed earlier, outlines the path forward for the U.S. nuclear force. Currently, the prognosis is for the nuclear force to continue on a qualitatively similar path, with marginal or evolutionary changes in capability. To be sure, planned reductions in the number of tubes on SSBN(X), or mounting single warheads on Minuteman III or its possible replacement, both make downward scaling more straightforward from a hardware standpoint. Indeed, with the reduced warhead loading, it also provides some headroom for uploading in a pinch. Absent a dramatic change in international relations at the global or regional level – and Iran remains a wild card in the Middle East – or a revolutionary increase in capability by another nation, there is little or no pressure to modify the balance of capabilities or try to recover a capability eliminated by previous decisions.

Nevertheless, it is prudent to have in mind plans to recover options as needed, or to attempt to preserve future options in ways that will be both politically supportable and manageable in terms of their escalatory impact internationally. In this section, we briefly consider historical examples of the box canyons, roach motels, and wrong turns of the title, as well as the lessons that might be gained for the future.

Regional, or Non-Strategic, vs Strategic Nuclear Weapons:
Is a Nuke a Nuke?

Although this is a topic deserving of more discussion, let us briefly sketch out some of the parameters that affect the deterrent, or military, significance of nuclear weapons. We can intuitively grasp the difference between <u>strategic</u> nuclear weapons, with global destructive reach, and <u>regional</u> or <u>non-strategic</u> weapons with shorter range and, in some cases, more specialized use (e.g., a nuclear torpedo). The manner in which they are, or would be, employed is also significant: <u>offensively</u>, <u>defensively</u>, or perhaps in the case of a country like Iran or North Korea, <u>non-traditionally</u> (colloquially, the "nuclear car bomb," delivered in a non-attributable fashion). *Where* is significant: <u>in-country</u> or <u>extra-territorial</u> use. Considering the combination of the manner and the location, clearly offensive use extra-territorially is far more threatening and escalatory than defensive use in-country, for example. Yield should make a difference, but perhaps less on first use than in multiple-use situations; and perhaps not much beyond <u>high</u> and <u>low</u> from the standpoint of the signal sent (where the fog of war would be expected to be significant in a conflict), although yield is much more significant from the standpoint of calculated military requirements.

The nature of the correspondents in a deterrence relationship is highly significant, too. Strategic depth is important: <u>big-sponge</u> countries such as the United States, Russia, and China have a much different strategic calculus, and present a different picture to potential adversaries, than <u>shallow-depth</u> countries such as Israel, Pakistan, or even a Japan. Relative strength of conventional military forces plays a role; intuitively it seems that the possession of non-strategic weapons in addition to <u>conventional superiority</u> is more threatening than the possession of such weapons by a <u>conventionally inferior</u> nation.

Indeed, in regard to this last point, considerable discussion has been devoted in recent years to the question of whether or not conventional weapons can assume certain deterrent roles currently filled by nuclear weapons.[1] We suspect that the deterrent capability of conventional weapons, in comparison to a nuclear option, depends at least as much on the conventional superiority or inferiority of the nations involved as it does on the weapons themselves. Indeed, in this regard, perhaps a certain "natural selection" has already been at work in the earlier elimination of some U.S. nuclear capabilities.

1. For example, see Michael S. Gerson, *Conventional Deterrence in the Second Nuclear Age*, *Parameters*, p. 32, Autumn 2009.

A Wrong Turn: The Reliable Replacement Warhead

Congressional funding for the Reliable Replacement Warhead first appeared in the Fiscal Year 2005 (FY05) federal budget, with the simple explanation that it was to be an effort "to improve the reliability, longevity, and certifiability of existing weapons and their components."[61] However, funding was zeroed in the FY09 budget, and in March 2009, the program was formally cancelled. In that short period of time, a design competition between the nuclear-weapons design laboratories was held and decided in favor of a team from the Lawrence Livermore National Laboratory (LLNL) and Sandia National Laboratories (SNL). Congress requested and received supporting studies from the JASON advisory group,[62,63] the Defense Science Board (DSB),[64] the American Association for the Advancement of Science (AAAS),[65] the National Academy of Sciences,[66] and a Congressional Commission on America's Strategic Posture.[67] Additionally, the National Nuclear Security Administration (NNSA) produced reports on a future nuclear-weapons production complex, a 2005 study[68] from the Secretary of Energy's Advisory Board (SEAB), and a Congressionally-mandated Complex 2030 report,[69] all to support production of a family of Reliable Replacement Warheads as well as Life Extension Programs of existing warheads, as necessary.

The issues surrounding RRW – a type of warhead, the first of which, the WR-1, was being developed by the LLNL/SNL team – were both technical and political. Technical issues provided the initial motivation: RRW was to be the embodiment of a design and production philosophy intended as an alternative to the continued life extension of weapons designed and first deployed during the Cold War. The Defense Science Board had declared indefinite life extension and remanufacture to be "clearly not a sustainable approach."[70] In the case of RRW, rather than optimizing warheads for maximum *specific yield*, the ratio of nuclear yield to warhead mass (measured in kilotons per kilogram), the basic strategy was to relax the requirement on specific yield and to capitalize on the greater mass allowable to increase design margins.** Thus, the WR-1 was to have the yield of the W76, which was mounted in the Mk-4 reentry vehicle, but it was to be mounted in the larger Mk-5 RV of the W88.[71] Derived from previously tested nuclear systems,[72] the redesigned RRW warheads were to provide for:

- Ease of production, surveillance (observation of warhead properties and performance), maintenance, and dismantlement;
- Reduced need for nuclear testing;
- Utilization of readily available, non-hazardous materials in their construction;
- Control of safety (the prevention of unexpected detonation) and surety (a measure of confidence that the warhead will operate as planned under all circumstances);
- Reductions in life-cycle cost targets; and
- Modularity.

Whatever the intended advantages of RRW and specifically WR-1, the advantages of the new approach embodied by RRW were less clear-cut than intended in comparison to the practice of conducting Life Extension Programs (LEPs) of tested, known nuclear weapons. Barry Hannah, Chair of the RRW Project Officers Group, a key programmatic element, expressed his opinion to a member of the Congressional Research Service that the competing W76-1 LEP would meet the Navy's needs and provide for an increase in design margins in the process of compensating for known problems or expected uncertainties.[73] Reviewers also noted that a new WR-1 would probably experience difficulties as a new system, with new production processes, that would take more time than expected to resolve. Substantial uncertainties about the ability of the existing NNSA nuclear weapons complex to produce new nuclear primaries, or pits, in the numbers required for a production run of WR-1 generated serious concern. When the FY08 budget eliminated funding for a Consolidated Plutonium Center to build new pits, while adding funding to explore the desirability of reusing existing pits in WR-1, the handwriting was on the wall.

Ultimately, the combination of political issues and unknown technical challenges were the undoing of RRW. The system was judged to be a "new" nuclear weapon, the introduction of which was regarded to be inconsistent with U.S. nonproliferation goals. Further, notwithstanding the fact that RRW was to be based on tested nuclear explosives and that its increased margins were intended to reduce the need for future nuclear testing, the fact that it was in some sense "untested," especially

---

** "Margin" is defined broadly for a number of nuclear design metrics, or key "performance gates," as the difference between the normal, or design, operating point for a key parameter and the threshold value for operation. As an example (see the National Academy of Sciences report in the reference), if the identified parameter is the yield of a nuclear-weapon primary, and if the metric is yield of the secondary driven by the primary, the margin is the difference between the minimum primary yield required to achieve acceptable secondary yield, and the (larger) primary yield at which the primary has been designed to operate.

in comparison with Cold War nuclear weapons, was regarded as a source of concern that it might create an impediment to ratification of the Comprehensive Test Ban Treaty (CTBT).

The *Final Report of the Congressional Commission on the Strategic Posture of the United States* provided a post mortem on the RRW, as well as a valuable lesson drawn from the experience:[74]

> *The two basic approaches to refurbishment and modernization are, in fact, not stark alternatives. Rather, they are options along a spectrum. That spectrum is defined at its two ends by the pure remanufacturing of existing warheads with existing components at one end and complete redesign and new production of all system components at the other. In between are various options to utilize existing components and design solutions as needed. Different warheads may lend themselves to different solutions along this spectrum.*
>
> ...
>
> *The commission recommends that Congress authorize NNSA to conduct a cost and feasibility study of incorporating enhanced safety, security, and reliability features in the second half of the planned W76 life extension program. This authorization should permit the design of specific components, including both pits and secondaries, as appropriate.*

A year later, the 2010 *Nuclear Posture Review Report* assimilated this recommendation in large part. Looking forward over the coming 30 years, the report reached four conclusions about the future lifetime extension of existing nuclear weapons. In addition to pledges not to resume nuclear testing and to pursue ratification of the CTBT, these conclusions included the following:[75]

- *The United States will not develop new nuclear warheads. Life Extension Programs (LEPs) will use only nuclear components based on previously tested designs, and will not support new military missions or provide for new military capabilities.*
- *The United States will study options for ensuring the safety, security, and reliability of nuclear warheads on a case-by-case basis, consistent with the congressionally mandated Stockpile Management Program. The full range of LEP approaches will be considered: refurbishment of existing warheads, reuse of nuclear components from different warheads, and replacement of nuclear components.*
- *In any decision to proceed to engineering development for warhead LEPs, the United States will give strong preference to options for refurbishment or reuse. Replacement of nuclear components would be undertaken only if critical Stockpile Management Program goals could not be otherwise met, and if specifically authorized by the President and approved by Congress.*

Although the report did not mention movement to larger RVs, as was the case with RRW moving from the Mk-4 to the larger Mk-5, and while it stated a preference for refurbishment or reuse, the policy was moved to somewhere between the two technical endpoints called out in 2009 by the Congressional Commission. Now, nuclear components based on previously tested nuclear designs can be used as replacements in future Life Extension Programs.

The lesson of the RRW experience for the nuclear force was that new systems, even new systems with the military capabilities of previous systems, are problematic; however, modifications of existing systems, or options that can be portrayed as modifications of existing systems, are possible, subject to the proper approvals. In this sense, the RRW represented a wrong turn, a direction not pursued, but only a wrong turn.

Along these lines, in late 2012, the Nuclear Weapons Council adopted a new framework, still not fully finalized, for the maintenance of U.S. nuclear warheads, the so-called "3+2" vision.[76] This plan would include three "interoperable" ballistic missile warheads and two nuclear weapons to be delivered by aircraft, a gravity bomb and an air-launched cruise missile. The interoperable ballistic missile warheads would be carried by either the Mk-5 RV for the Trident-II SLBM or the Mk-21 RV for the Minuteman III ICBM. Both RVs could carry one of three nuclear-explosive packages (NEPs) integrated with non-nuclear systems that maximize the use of common and adaptable components. The first such interoperable warhead, the IW-1, is being developed with a design based on the melding of the existing W78 and W88-1 designs. Future warheads, the IW-2 and IW-3 are projected at this time to be based on the life extension of the W87 and W88 (IW-2) and the W76-1 (IW-3). The air-delivered systems are currently expected to employ the B61-12 warhead for the gravity bomb, while a final decision for the cruise missile warhead has not yet been made.

According to a Pentagon official,[77] the 3+2 plan will result in reductions to (1) the number of warhead types, from seven to five; (2) the current heavy reliance on the W76; and (3) the overall stockpile size, because of the reduced requirement for non-deployed hedge warheads. It is hoped that the cost of warhead life extension and maintenance can be reduced, although it was admitted that DoD costs for the testing of the newly-loaded RVs could offset any savings. Finally, the plan is expected to help maintain nuclear design skills by presenting a greater challenge than a life-extension program based on the refurbishment of existing warheads.

An Historical Roach Motel: SRAM T vs the B61

As described earlier in the report, development of new versions of the Short-Range Attack Missile was underway at the end of the Cold War: SRAM II (AGM-131A), to be carried by heavy bombers and armed with the W89 warhead, and SRAM T (see **Figure 11**), to be carried by the F-15E and armed with the W91 warhead. As recounted in a 1991 GAO report, serious problems, primarily with engine development, pushed SRAM II years behind schedule and caused costs to balloon, even following reductions in required performance criteria.[78] This was the context in which SRAM II and SRAM T were cancelled as part of the PNIs of 1991 and 1992.[79] Nevertheless, in announcing that cancellation, President Bush promised to retain "an effective air-delivered nuclear capability in Europe." Today, this role is filled by the B61 gravity bomb, some still stationed in Europe, to be delivered by T-DCA; in addition, B61s and the B83 bomb, as well as ALCMs, can be delivered by heavy bombers.

In fact, SRAM II/T was cancelled over 20 years ago. The issue today is not the missile itself, but rather the capability a missile like it would represent: a nuclear-armed supersonic standoff missile carried by T-DCA, F-16s or Tornados today, and F-35 in the future. Such a missile, with the standoff it offers for the delivery vehicle, would arguably be superior in military capability to a B61, which requires the delivering aircraft to penetrate essentially to within sight of the target. Further, pointing back to Table 1, we see that except for the large differences in weight between B61 and SRAM II, the two have quite similar physical dimensions, possibly allowing the use of the same warhead for

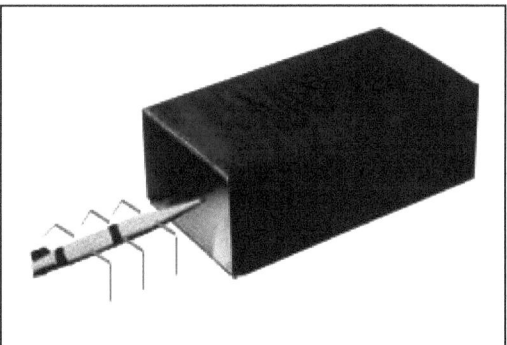

Figure 11. SRAM T enters the Roach Motel.

both and simplifying the task of modifying the delivery platform to carry a similar standoff missile.

Of course, the case study of RRW shows that military effectiveness is not the only factor affecting the desirability of developing a modern nuclear-armed short-range standoff missile (which we abbreviate N-SRSO) for tactical delivery. Indeed, circumstances have placed such a system in our so-called Roach Motel: it's gotten in, but under current circumstances, it is very unlikely to get out, for the following reasons:

- As we noted earlier, the current nuclear force appears to be up to the task of meeting U.S. deterrence requirements for the foreseeable future. In this case, development of a modern N-SRSO would probably be rejected as a "new," and likely superior, military capability even if it were deployed as a one-for-one replacement for B61. In this light, one could expect to see such a missile viewed as a threat to regional and strategic stability, a stumbling block for future arms control negotiations, and inconsistent with U.S. nonproliferation policy.
- B61 has become a visible symbol of the nuclear element of the NATO alliance, and the development of a new U.S. tactical nuclear weapon would likely stimulate considerable discussion within the alliance that would revive controversial issues raised at the 2010 NATO Lisbon Summit, and resolved in NATO's *2010 Strategic Concept.*
- Substantial investment is being made in the Life Extension Program for B61, projected to be US$10B as of July 2012, according to Senator Dianne Feinstein.[80] It is unlikely that B61 would be replaced for some time, or that an additional tactical nuclear weapon would be developed at additional cost, except in the face of a significant new military requirement.
- Finally, an N-SRSO would have to offer a capability not provided by LRSO delivered by B-52H or a future LRS-B bomber.

Given the shorter range of the delivery aircraft, tactical N-SRSO would be most effective if based regionally; however, this would pose political and logistical challenges. Permanent basing in all but NATO countries presents political or regional stability difficulties, discussed earlier. Temporary basing in time of elevated tensions would doubtless affect the level of tension, which becomes part of the calculus for doing so: Are the United States and its allies willing to pay the price for the elevated tensions? Is the signaling of moving an N-SRSO into the region actually a desirable outcome? One can see that temporary basing provides less flexibility for decision makers. Beyond the political-military issues, the logistics are demanding: it would be necessary to establish facilities with the necessary security and hardness to meet nuclear requirements.

Enhanced military capability alone would not justify development of an N-SRSO. Some combination of circumstances, most likely outside the Euro-Atlantic region, requiring a regional capability not provided by strategic ballistic missiles or LRSO that both deters adversaries and assures allies and partners would be the likely core motivation.

A Possible Box Canyon? A Low-Yield Version of the W76 SLBM Warhead

Recently,[81] Elbridge Colby argued that U.S. interests are best served by the inclusion of a nuclear capability that is "limited, discriminate, and evidently restrained." Considering the economic constraints, evaluating the alternatives among existing systems, and drawing on a suggestion by Ambassador Linton Brooks, he recommended that the best current option is a low-yield version of the W76 warhead carried on the Trident II SLBM. In his evaluation, the overflight issue for ICBMs is problematic, and the passage of time and development of defensive technologies has reduced the reliability of current delivery aircraft, B2 and T-DCA carrying gravity bombs and B-52 delivering ALCMs. Looking to the future, he recommended a defense-penetrating LRSO as likely a preferable option.

The point made by Colby was that effective nuclear deterrence that serves the interests of both the United States and its allies requires more than the single-minded pursuit of the goal of preventing all nuclear-weapons use. Rather, he wrote that such a limited strategy creates a vulnerability of its own and raises a question among U.S. allies about the resolve underpinning extended deterrence, a point notably made by German Chancellor Helmut Schmidt in a 1977 lecture.[82] Colby argued that this creates a need, in effect, for additional rungs at the bottom of the escalation ladder to allow for the limited, discriminate demonstration that a conflict involves issues of sufficient national-security import that further pursuit could lead to a mutually disastrous nuclear exchange.

His desire for a de-escalatory demonstration capability mirrors in some important respects a lengthy public discussion conducted in the Russian military-theoretical literature during the 1990s, accompanied by shifts in Russian nuclear doctrine.[83] Russian authors there generally favored, and fleshed out, a doctrine of limited use of nuclear weapons –drawing on Russia's greater breadth of non-strategic options as well as single-warhead ICBMs – in demonstration strikes aimed at preventing regional conflicts, nuclear or otherwise, from evolving to large-scale conflicts. Russian interest at that point was motivated more by the survival of the Russian state under conditions of acknowledged conventional inferiority, than by the credibility of any extended-deterrence commitments.

We would expand the discussion a bit to recognize evolving deterrence requirements that appear to differ at the global and regional levels. Returning to a point made more than once here, the 2010 *Nuclear Posture Review Report* set dual goals of maintaining both strategic deterrence and stability on the one hand, and regional deterrence and assurance of allies and partners on the other. Looking forward from the present, we have noted that the United States has global deterrence relationships with Russia and China, as well as regional relationships that include (but are not limited to) Russia in the Euro-Atlantic and Western Pacific regions, and China in the Western Pacific. Both Russia and China possess non-strategic nuclear-weapon options more specialized to regional deterrence. On the other hand, emerging regional powers with more primitive, lower-yield nuclear weapons create the possibility of self-deterrence by the United States, or reduced responsiveness, created by a deficit of "proportionate" U.S. response options.

The arguments against the development of a low-yield SLBM warhead are easy to anticipate: a "new" military capability, a "more usable" nuclear weapon, lack of a requirement based on current relations among the nuclear powers. This last point was anticipated by Colby, with the counter that events could strain the capabilities of a system developed for the Cold War.

Could a low-yield warhead option for Trident II create a box canyon for future development, from which the United States would wish to walk back at some point in the not-so-distant future? The point of course is whether there is a need for a "limited, discriminate, and evidently restrained" option either to manage escalation with a global nuclear power, or to provide a "proportionate" retaliatory response – deterrence by punishment – for an emergent regional nuclear power. In the event that the answer to either is yes, the next question is whether a low-yield warhead delivered by an SLBM, likely the shortest route to developing such a capability, is the preferred option. Beyond the new-capability or usability arguments, we suggest that the desirability of adopting this option hinges on two factors.

First, if deterrence fails, can U.S. decision makers expect that the detonation of a lower-yield SLBM warhead will be recognized as such on the appropriate time scales? We propose that the immediate reaction to any nuclear detonation will be the recognition of massive destruction and the detection of nuclear fallout. With no visual sense of scale for destruction beyond that provided by aging photos of Hiroshima and Nagasaki, the fog of war could well obscure, on times scales appropriate to decision making under fire, the difference between a low-yield W76 and the higher-yield options carried by the same missile. The determination of yield could trail by days the decision on response. Thus,

- The availability of the option itself will likely have a useful deterrent effect, especially as a swift-and-sure, proportionate retaliatory response to an emergent regional nuclear power.
- As a responsive, second-use retaliatory option, with some expectation of the scale of a response, the low yield is possibly more likely to be perceived as such.
- Conversely, at the onset of a conflict, at the point at which a pre-emptive low-yield demonstration of resolve is required, whatever the provocation, the low yield is less likely to be recognized on a time scale appropriate to the decision making of the recipient. In other words, the message of "evidently restrained" is much less likely to be received.

Second, how does the ambiguity accompanying the use of an otherwise strategic system – an SLBM – affect its value as an element of extended deterrence? To be sure, TLAM/N, a submarine-launched cruise missile with greater available yield than the low-yield W76 in question, was judged by U.S. allies to be an acceptable instrument of extended deterrence. Therefore, this question focuses on the expected response to the use of an SLBM.

This last issue is a key one as we look to an uncertain future: are there regional-deterrence situations in which the message sent by the availability of non-strategic options is more appropriate? Alternatively, in the way that basing of non-strategic U.S. weapons in Europe sent, and continues to send, an intended message about U.S. commitment, does U.S. reliance on strategic systems even for extended deterrence send the same message in other regions? Finally, if deterrence fails – a low-probability, high-consequence event – does the availability of only strategic options provide the necessary range of options and flexibility in order to best serve the interests of the United States and its allies?

The future use of LRSO in this role may be more desirable, as suggested by Colby. Heavy bombers are essentially a dual-capable system, even if they are counted – in unique fashion – under New START. Nevertheless, the desirability of this option could change dramatically if bombers were one half of a future strategic dyad.

Final Thoughts: Options for the Future

Before we close, we emphasize three points about the discussion in this section:

- The current path for U.S. nuclear-force development points to a future force qualitatively similar to the force of today: a nuclear triad plus a gravity bomb delivered by T-DCA.

- Although perhaps not ideally suited to all possible anticipated global and regional deterrence situations, the current force is adequate, and foreseeable circumstances do not demand markedly different capabilities.
- Nuclear-force considerations are an element of a broader U.S. national-security policy that supports nonproliferation and arms control by aiming for the reduction of the role for, and the numbers of, nuclear weapons.

This context does not currently call for the development of new nuclear missions or weapons, although modifications that maintain the safety, security, and effectiveness of the existing arsenal are allowed. Nevertheless, we consider the kinds of changes in the security environment, alternative futures, that might necessitate the development of new capabilities in the nuclear force.

Evaluating the Circumstances for Deterrence and Use in Case Deterrence Fails

The point of this section is to consider options that might be needed under future conditions significantly different from those expected today. In the study of *Concepts of Analysis for Nuclear Strategy*, Daryl Press outlined the three features of such alternative futures most likely to have a top-level effect on nuclear-force requirements:[84]

- The relative conventional military strength of the United States;
- Relations between the major nuclear powers (or Great Powers); and
- The extent of proliferation of nuclear weapons and the strength of the nonproliferation regime.

A significant deterioration of the international situation in one or more of these realms might generate the need for different nuclear-force postures or capabilities.

The purposes to which a nuclear nation would put nuclear weapons, and the types of nuclear weapon, are also a factor in considering the possibility of a change in the nuclear force. Along the lines of an introductory discussion of these issues in a text box some pages back, we consider the following, somewhat loosely-defined qualitative criteria:

- The circumstances of possible use:
  - Offensive (in support of an expansionist objective) vs defensive (in response to an attack) vs non-traditional (the aforementioned "nuclear car bomb," creating a particularly difficult situation, since response is tied up with the challenging business of attribution of the source).
  - In-country by the user of the nuclear weapon (expected to be a defensive use) vs extra-territorially (in which case use could be offensive or defensive).
- The relative characterization of the combatants:
  - Great strategic depth (so-called "big sponge" countries capable of absorbing at least a limited nuclear strike and continuing to function) vs shallow strategic depth (a country for which even a single nuclear strike, or a limited number against a few predominant concentrations of population or industry, would be very difficult to absorb).
  - Conventionally-superior militarily vs conventionally-inferior.
- The nature of the weapons:
  - High-yield (approaching a hundred kilotons or more) vs low yield (up to about twenty kilotons).

- o Strategic systems capable of delivery from intercontinental range (delivered by an ICBM or SLBM, or perhaps delivered by a heavy bomber, although this latter is more ambiguously "strategic") vs non-strategic systems that deliver over shorter range, regional or theater.
- o Alternatively, for some nations, strategic systems may be those capable of hitting large-area targets (which some would call counter-value or large-scale counter-force), while non-strategic systems may be those intended for battlefield use.

Considering the Possible Options

<u>Strategic Deterrence</u>

The core of U.S. strategic deterrence remains the nuclear triad. A 2009 analysis of current and projected versions of the triad, as well as a comparison of the triad to an SSBN/SLBM-only monad or all possible dyads (SSBN/SLBM + ICBMs, SSBN/SLBM + bombers, ICBMs + bombers) can be found in the article by Johnson, Bowie, and Haffa.[85]

Single-warhead ICBMs and the reduced number of missiles projected for the successor to the *Ohio*-class SSBNs provide for easier downward scaling if desired, offer some upload potential if circumstances dictate, and have some of the key attributes of a more stable nuclear force called for by the 1983 President's Commission on Strategic Forces.[86]

Two options under consideration for a future Ground-Based Strategic Deterrent – mobility and adaptability to carry trajectory-shaping or trajectory-correcting vehicles – could address two challenges confronting ICBMs: increased survivability and the issue of ICBM-launched warheads overflying Russia to reach non-Russian targets of potential interest.

<u>Regional Deterrence</u>

Regional deterrence, on the other hand, is becoming a more complex problem. The associated issues in an age of emerging nuclear states or global nuclear powers with far less limited objectives than world domination are more complex than those of Cold-War strategic deterrence. Of course, Cold War deterrence involved subtleties appropriate to the age: we recall Garthoff's observation that the number of warheads on U.S. INF-range missile systems was less than the number on similar Soviet systems in order to signal that escalation to the global level was still possible.

Consider as examples the following three deterrence situations that United States decision makers could face in possible alternative futures:

- <u>In-country, defensive use of nuclear weapons by an adversary</u>. Imagine that a nuclear-armed adversary badly miscalculates and attacks a U.S. ally, and the United States responds with superior conventional force. Imagine also that in the face of a perceived threat to regime survival, this nuclear-armed adversary considers the in-country, defensive use of nuclear weapons against U.S. and allied forces. If the international community perceives that the threat of such use alone inhibits U.S. actions, this could constitute an insult to the nonproliferation regime. We are reminded of the comparisons of Ghaddafi's Libya to Kim's North Korea (which are typically made without consideration of the relative sizes of the two nations' militaries, the vastly different terrain in each country, and the conventional artillery threat to South Korea's capital). Even worse, if actual nuclear use by an adversary blunted a U.S. and allied assault, making it in some sense "successful," the damage to the nonproliferation regime is enormous.

- <u>Reassurance of U.S. allies with limited strategic depth threatened by an emergent nuclear power</u>. An extreme example of the former would be Israel or the Gulf States under the threat of a nuclear Iran. Less extreme is South Korea, with the concentration of population and government within conventional artillery range of the demilitarized zone, or Japan, with the high concentration of population and industry near Tokyo and Osaka. For Japan, this factor was recognized in Japanese analyses of its security situation.[87,88] Reassurance of such allies depends on the maintenance of a swift and sure retaliatory capability. However, the threat of retaliation must be backed with not only the resolve to employ it in the defense of U.S. allies, but also defensive capabilities and very clear messaging and responsive capability in the event that an attack seems imminent. Simultaneous reassurance and deterrence presents special challenges.[††]

- <u>Extraterritorial, non-strategic, offensive use of nuclear weapons in support of limited military objectives against a U.S. ally</u>. The United States has Cold War-era experience in deterring large-scale conflict with an implacable, ideologically-opposed enemy backed by strategic nuclear capability. The demise of the Soviet Union has lowered the geopolitical and military stakes dramatically. However, in an alternate future in which relations with Russia declined precipitously (for reasons one cannot foresee today), one could imagine that limited military actions on the Russian periphery would be supported by the implicit threat of non-strategic nuclear weapons. Indeed, positioning and posturing such weapons to manipulate periphery states by the threat alone would constitute a threat to regional stability.

Before we consider the options for facing threats such as these, we offer two observations about the future of regional deterrence. First, we address a commonly asked question: Can conventional weapons replace nuclear weapons in accomplishing at least some deterrence missions?[89] Our reply is that the United States has been making these kinds of replacements continuously, during and after the Cold War. Since the high point of U.S. nuclear war planning during the Cold War, the United States has eliminated all of its non-strategic naval and ground-launched nuclear weapons, its nuclear artillery, land mines, and ballistic missile defense system, and its air-to-air missiles. Nevertheless, the *2010 Nuclear Posture Review Report* pointed to a more focused role for the remaining U.S. nuclear weapons: "The fundamental role of U.S. nuclear weapons … is to deter nuclear attack on the United States, our allies, and partners." That formulation – "fundamental role" – is to be distinguished from the more restrictive role that did not make it into the Review, "sole purpose," a point discussed in a recent paper by Brad Roberts, former Deputy Assistant Secretary of Defense for Nuclear and Missile Defense Policy.[90] In this spirit, U.S. non-strategic weapons should exist for the primary, but not necessarily sole, purpose of deterring the use of nuclear weapons, or other weapons of mass destruction, by our adversaries. That includes *first* use as well as *further* use; i.e., subsequent use after the initiation of nuclear conflict, a situation perhaps more accurately characterized as *escalation control*, a subject beyond our scope here.

Our second observation is that, in thinking of possible alternative futures, planners must structure a nuclear force for strategic stability, as well as regional nuclear deterrence if possible, and escalation control if necessary. This brings to mind three points:

[††] Indeed, allies as well as adversaries apply a worst-case analysis to their security situation, which causes allies to minimize the capability meant to assure them, while adversaries magnify the same capability, a situation meant to be moderated through regular consultation with the recipients of extended deterrence.

- Schelling's aforementioned description of deterrence in terms of "the exploitation of potential force."
- Colby's admonition that making prevention of nuclear use the only goal creates its own vulnerability.
- Kenneth Waltz' comment: "If countries armed with nuclear weapons go to war, they do so knowing that their suffering may be unlimited. ... In a conventional world, one is uncertain about winning or losing. In a nuclear world, one is uncertain about surviving or being annihilated."[91]

In this vein, we compare the wide diversity of Russia's non-strategic nuclear force to the limited non-strategic options available to the United States. Russia admits to its current conventional inferiority to NATO. Further, given Russia's long borders and lack of offensive conventional strength, those non-strategic nuclear forces are less threatening in providing a range of last-resort defensive options than they would be if Russia were an offensive threat with superior conventional capability. On the other hand, in view of the conventional superiority of the U.S. military, a similar non-strategic U.S. nuclear arsenal would be far more threatening; however, the United States must have sufficient capability to deter offensive non-strategic nuclear use and control nuclear escalation if first use occurs.

The challenge of deterring regional nuclear threats could be addressed in part by the following adaptations of existing strategic systems:

- A low-yield SLBM warhead, as discussed by Colby. This offers (1) reliable defense penetration, (2) rapid retaliatory response, and (3) a proportionate response against new nuclear powers not yet possessing high-yield weapons of their own – provided the low-yield option on an otherwise high-yield system is discerned. A swift and sure retaliatory capability is particularly valuable in deterring regional adversaries and reassuring allies with limited strategic depth. In response to the possible counter argument that a low-yield system is more "usable," we argue that the possibility of U.S. self-deterrence due to an unwillingness to respond at the substantially higher yield of current SLBM warheads actually makes deterrence less effective, increasing the possibility for nuclear use by an adversary.
- A limited strike with ALCM or LRSO in the future, this latter mentioned by Colby also as a possibly more desirable option than the low-yield SLBM. Presumably these weapons can offer a proportionate response, and they have pinpoint accuracy; however, defense penetration is more challenging for a cruise missile, and response is slowed by the longer flight times (hours as opposed to tens of minutes). With regard to the longer flight time, a heavy bomber with a full load of cruise missiles on the loose is a very flexible option for the user that nevertheless offers a very sobering prospect for the adversary until it becomes clear how many of those cruise missiles are going to be released.

The common disadvantage of these systems is the uncertain message sent by the low-yield employment of a strategic weapon also capable of operation in a high-yield mode. The two immediate observables following a nuclear detonation are the enormous destruction and the accompanying radiation. Although the destruction at high yields could be orders of magnitude larger than that of the low-yield option, few eyes are calibrated to quickly detect the difference. Careful analysis would "prove" the difference, but in the political atmosphere surrounding nuclear conflict, "proof" is heavily influenced by the desired conclusion of the parties involved.

For similar reasons, and because of the increased confusion in wartime that Colby acknowledges, we are skeptical of the utility of low-yield, discriminate options in a signaling or de-escalatory role. To be sure, one can find substantial support for this nuclear role in the Russian defense-analysis literature, but perhaps the best reason one could find on the U.S. side for developing such an option would be the possibility of deterring or limiting its use by an adversary.

The remaining option now available is nuclear-armed heavy bombers or T-DCA armed with B61 gravity bombs. This latter option is an element of the glue holding NATO together as a nuclear alliance. This option requires in-theater storage of nuclear weapons, either permanently – the current case in Europe – or temporarily. Further, armed with B61s, T-DCA are required to penetrate an integrated air-defense system basically to within visual range of the target, drop their ordnance, and then fly back to friendly territory.

Looking forward, if regional or global security were to deteriorate to the point that another, or better, regional nuclear deterrent capability were required, it seems that either some kind of short-range standoff missile for T-DCA or a resurrected submarine-launched cruise missile are likely options. As we discuss in the Appendix, there are multiple options for a short-range standoff missile (our aforementioned N-SRSO). Basically, the end points for N-SRSO technology are speed – either supersonic or hypersonic – and stealth, with the optimal solution likely somewhere in between. As we showed earlier in Table 1, the long-retired SRAM II – an example of a supersonic rocket – was quite similar in size to the B61, although given the high density of the rocket propellant, it was almost three times the weight. As discussed in the Appendix, the negative for hypersonic systems, which use air-breathing "scramjet" engines, is the large size that accompanies both the rocket booster they require to reach the speeds necessary for the scramjet engine to operate and the fuel they must carry (at much lower density, and thus higher volume, than solid rocket propellant). Stealth, however, as discussed by Letsinger, may be an asset of diminishing value, unless combined with at least supersonic speed, due to improvements in radar systems and processing directed against it.[92]

Finally, we consider the resurrection of submarine-launched cruise missiles such as TLAM/N. To return to our earlier discussion, they offer in-theater basing without the challenges of foreign basing; however, on a submarine, they offer little in the way of visible strategic message once the submarine is deployed. Potentially, submarine basing in-theater shortens the response time relative to ALCM or LRSO on bombers based in the United States, and it offers substantial advantage in weapons security over temporary T-DCA basing. The nuclear explosive is essentially that provided by ALCM or LRSO, though, so there is little or no functional advantage there. Thus, it appears that a new submarine-launched cruise missile would offer advantages in potentially improved non-strategic response time and weapon security, but the disadvantages of little visible strategic messaging and the growing danger of exposure of the submarine's location when it launches.

Appendix: Options for Future Regional Nuclear Deterrent Capabilities

Possible future options for a range of nuclear deterrent capabilities – strategic and regional – can be divided first into those that are modifications of strategic nuclear-weapon systems and those that would be non-strategic nuclear weapons. In the former class, for regional application, we discussed a low-yield SLBM warhead option and use of an air-launched cruise missile – ALCM today, LRSO in the future. In addition, it is possible that options considered for delivery by surface-launched missile boosters for Conventional Prompt Global Strike might be adapted for use in either a strategic or regional nuclear deterrent role.[93]

The Defense Advanced Research Projects Agency (DARPA) and the U.S. Army have both tested unpowered hypersonic boost-glide vehicles. The concept involves the use of a surface-launched missile to boost a hypersonic glide vehicle to an elevation above the atmosphere, from which it reenters the atmosphere at high velocity and performs non-ballistic maneuvers to achieve cross range and glide range well beyond the capacities of ballistic reentry vehicles. The missile can be either an ICBM or SLBM devoted to non-nuclear weapon delivery to strategic ranges.

- DARPA's project was the more ambitious; as part of its FALCON program (Force Application and Launch from Continental United States), two flight tests of the Hypersonic Test Vehicle (HTV-2) were conducted in 2010 and 2011. According to DARPA, the second flight test demonstrated "stable aerodynamically controlled flight" at speeds up to Mach 20. Flight was terminated due to unexpectedly rapid degradation of the flight surfaces.[94] A third flight test was cancelled as DARPA shifted its focus from strategic hypersonic applications to tactical hypersonic missions.[95]
- The U.S. Army's Advanced Hypersonic Weapon (AHW)[96] employs the Sandia National Laboratory's Sandia Winged Energetic Reentry Vehicle Experiment (SWERVE) reentry technology demonstrator concept.[97] This concept involves the integration of an unpowered conical aeroshell with strakes and flaperons used to alter the direction of flight and impose and maintain an aerodynamic angle-of-attack to generate lift. The AHW achieves hypersonic speeds via a large missile booster (ICBM or SLBM class) and uses active controls to perform reentry maneuvers and glide to the target, depositing kinetic energy onto its target. In a 2011 test flight, an AHW missile/maneuvering-vehicle system employing a three-stage booster successfully flew 2,000 kilometers from Kauai to Kwajalein. However, an AHW does not possess nearly the aerodynamic efficiency of an HTV-2, starkly reducing its glide and cross range capacity versus HTV-2.

Despite the intricate shapes of aerodynamic vehicles like the HTV-2, their lack of propulsion prevents them from matching the cross range or glide range of hypersonic scramjet systems exemplified by the X-43 or X-51A.[98] Delivery vehicles with propulsion systems that do not carry their own oxidizer are known as "airbreathers." They operate at extreme velocity and have large cross- and glide-range capacity versus a ballistic RV, due to their ability to maintain velocity while maneuvering.[99] The X-51A Waverider was flight tested in May 2013.[100] Released from a B-52 at 50,000 feet and a speed of Mach 0.8, the solid booster of the ATACMS (Army Tactical Missile System) accelerated the X-51A scramjet to Mach 4.9 and an elevation of 63,000 feet. At that point, the booster fell away, and the X-51A flew for an additional 210 seconds, climbing to 64,000 feet and reaching a speed of Mach 5.1, at which point it exhausted its fuel while still accelerating. The test system is shown in **Figure 12**. The scramjet (white) is forward, extending back to the small wings; aft of that is the inter-stage, followed by the gray ATACMS booster. According to the Air Force, the X-51A has a length of 7.6 meters (4.3 meters for the scramjet-powered cruiser on the front end, 1.5 meters for the interstage, and 1.8 meters for the booster), and the mass of the whole system is about 1,820 kilograms.[101] Its range is specified to be over 720 kilometers, its top speed is Mach 6, and its operating ceiling is over 21,000 meters. The X-51 is intended to provide the basis for development of the High-Speed Strike Weapon (HSSW), which is to be deliverable by the B-2 and F-35.

The obvious intended advantage of the proposed HSSW over the SRAM II, which was cancelled by the first Bush administration, is speed: Mach 6 vs Mach 2+. Additionally, the X-51 range of over 700 kilometers is almost double the expected 400 kilometers of SRAM II. However, an HSSW, with its scramjet, interstage, and rocket booster engine is much more complex, heavier, and longer than the two-pulse solid rocket of the SRAM II. Indeed, while the SRAM II was to have room to carry a nuclear warhead, the X-51 appears to have inadequate room for the explosive.

Figure 12. X-51A "stack," under the wing of a B-52. *Air Force photo.*

The alternative to speed for evading defenses is of course stealth. Stealthy cruise missiles, like Boeing's JABMM (Joint Air-Breathing Multi-Role Missile)[7] or Lockheed's JASSM (Joint Air-to-Surface Stand-off Missile),[102] can ideally reach targets before detection, or delay detection and targeting sufficiently that the defensive systems cannot take out the incoming cruise missile. Stealth becomes important given the rapid advancement of air defense networks when coupled to the cruise missile's moderate speed. Cruise missiles represent the simplest technological option, but like the HSSW and SRAM, a cruise missile requires its carrier to transit to the weapon dispense point. And, the cruise missile flies at less than one-fifth the speed of the attack missile, and less than one-twentieth of the HTV-2.

References

[1]   Remarks by Rose Gottemoeller, Acting Under Secretary for Arms Control and International Security, *Exchange Monitor's Fifth Annual Nuclear Deterrence Summit*, 21 February 2013, Arlington, VA, available from the IIP Digital website managed by the U.S. State Department, http://iipdigital.usembassy.gov/st/english/texttrans/2013/02/20130221142871.html#ixzz2QZjgcwzH.

[2]   President Barack Obama, *Remarks by President Obama at the Brandenburg Gate -- Berlin, Germany*, 19 June 2013, available from the White House website http://www.whitehouse.gov/the-press-office/2013/06/19/remarks-president-obama-brandenburg-gate-berlin-germany.

[3]   *The Nuclear Posture Review Report*, April 2010, available from the U.S. Department of Defense website, http://www.defense.gov/npr/docs/2010%20nuclear%20posture%20review%20report.pdf.

[4]   *The Nuclear Posture Review Report*, April 2010, available from the U.S. Department of Defense website, http://www.defense.gov/npr/docs/2010%20nuclear%20posture%20review%20report.pdf.

[5]   U.S. Department of Defense, *Moscow Treaty: Article-by-Article Analysis*, available online from http://www.acq.osd.mil/tc/treaties/sort/sort_axa.htm.

[6]   *Fact Sheet, Increasing Transparency in the U.S. Nuclear Stockpile*, 3 May 2010, available from the U.S. Department of Defense website, http://www.defense.gov/npr/docs/10-05-03_fact_sheet_us_nuclear_transparency__final_w_date.pdf.

[7]   *New START Treaty Aggregate Numbers of Strategic Offensive Arms*, 3 April 2013, Bureau of Arms Control, Verification, and Compliance.

[8] S. Koch, *The Presidential Nuclear Initiatives of 1991-1992*, September 2012, National Defense University Press; see Appendix 1 for the texts of all initiatives.

[9] S. Koch, *The Presidential Nuclear Initiatives of 1991-1992*, September 2012, National Defense University Press; see Appendix 1 for the texts of all initiatives.

[10] President George H.W. Bush, *Address to the Nation on Reducing United States and Soviet Nuclear Weapons*, 27 September 1991, available from the website of the George Bush Presidential Library and Museum, http://bushlibrary.tamu.edu/research/public_papers.php?id=3438&year=1991&month=9.

[11] President George H.W. Bush, *State of the Union Address*, January 28, 1992, available online from http://millercenter.org/president/speeches/detail/5531.

[12] Redacted and declassified version of State Department cable 247871, 21 September 1979, *HLG: US Draft Report*, summarized and available through the website of The National Security Archive of George Washington University, http://www.gwu.edu/~nsarchiv/nukevault/ebb301/#6.

[13] R. L. Garthoff, *Détente and Confrontation: U.S.-Soviet Relations from Nixon to Reagan*, Washington, D.C., Brookings Institution, 1994.

[14] *Treaty Between The United States Of America And The Union Of Soviet Socialist Republics On The Elimination Of Their Intermediate-Range And Shorter-Range Missiles (INF Treaty): Narrative*, available from the U.S. Department of State website, http://www.state.gov/t/avc/trty/102360.htm#text.

[15] See, for example, L. Hughes, "Why Japan Will Not Go Nuclear (Yet), International and Domestic Constraints on the Nuclearization of Japan," *International Security*, vol. 31, no. 4, pp. 67-96, Spring 2007.

[16] *Boeing AGM-69 'SRAM*,'" available from http://www.strategic-air-command.com/missiles/Aircraft-Launched_Missiles/agm-69_SRAM_missile htm.

[17] Government Accountability Office (GAO), *Justification for the Short Range Attack Missile II*, December 1987, GAO/NSIAD-88-81B.

[18] *AGM-131*, Directory of U.S. Military Rockets and Missiles, http://www.designation-systems net/dusrm/m-131 html.

[19] GAO, *Unclassified Summary of GAO's SRAM II/T Classified Report*, enclosure to a GAO memo to Defense Secretary Aspin, 24 February 1992, GAO/NSIAD-92-145R.

[20] *Vice Adm Timothy Keating Briefing via Satellite-Teleconference from Bahrain*, 12 April 2003, News Transcript released by the Office of the Assistant Secretary of Defense for Public Affairs, available from http://www.defense.gov/transcripts/transcript.aspx?transcriptid=2370.

[21] Photograph : Mehdi Fedouach/AFP/Getty Images. March 29, 2003, Buyukmerdes, Turkey; credited by Jeffrey Lewis, *Why the Navy Should Retire TLAM/N*, 13 December 2009, *The Arms Control Wonk*, available from http://lewis.armscontrolwonk.com/archive/2560/why-the-navy-should-retire-tlam-n.

[22] *America's Strategic Posture; The Final Report of the Congressional Commission on the Strategic Posture of the United States*, 2009, U.S. Institute of Peace Press, Washington, DC, available from the Institute of Peace website, http://www.usip.org/files/America's_Strategic_Posture_Auth_Ed.pdf.

[23] An unofficial translation of the original Japanese-language letter is available from the Citizens' Nuclear Information Center, http://icnndngojapan files.wordpress.com/2010/01/20091224_okada_letter_en.pdf.

[24] *Joint Communique, The 42nd Meeting of the U.S.-ROK Security Consultative Meeting*, October 8, 2010, Washington, DC, available from the Department of Defense website, http://www.defense.gov/news/d20101008usrok.pdf.

[25] Joint Statement issued at the conclusion of the June 21, 2011 U.S.-Japan Security Consultative Committee meeting, attended by Secretary of State Hillary Rodham Clinton, Secretary of Defense Robert M. Gates, Minister for Foreign Affairs Matsumoto, and Minister of Defense Kitazawa, *Toward a Deeper and Broader U.S.-Japan Alliance: Building on 50 Years of Partnership*, available from the State Department website, http://www.state.gov/r/pa/prs/ps/2011/06/166597 htm.

[26] *Martin Marietta LGM-118A 'Peacekeeper' ICBM Fact Sheet*, available at the Hill AFB website, http://www.hill.af.mil/library/factsheets/factsheet.asp?id=5762, posted 19-Oct-2010.

[27] Steven A. Pomeroy, *Echoes That Never Were: American Mobile Intercontinental Ballistic Missiles, 1956-1983*, doctoral dissertation, Auburn University, 14 April 2006, report no. CI04-1762.

[28] See, for example, Art Hobson, *The ICBM Basing Question, Science and Global Security*, vol. 2, pp. 152-198, 1991.

[29] Steven A. Pomeroy, *Echoes That Never Were: American Mobile Intercontinental Ballistic Missiles, 1956-1983*, doctoral dissertation, Auburn University, 14 April 2006, report no. CI04-1762.

[30] *All It Touched off Was a Debate*, opinion by Fred Kaplan, published 18-Sep-2005, available at the New York Times website at http://www.nytimes.com/2005/09/18/weekinreview/18kaplan.html?pagewanted=all&_r=0.

[31] *Unarmed Midgetman Missile a Failure in First Test*, Andrew Rosenthal, New York Times, published 12-May-1989.

[32] *Modernizing U.S. Strategic Offensive Forces: Costs, Effects, and Alternatives*, Congressional Budget Office, November 1987, pg. *Summary xix.*

[33] *Historical Overview of the Space and Missile Systems Center, 1954-2003*, United States Air Force, available through the Los Angeles AFB website at http://www.losangeles.af mil/shared/media/document/AFD-120802-071.pdf.

[34] *U.S. Air Force Fact Sheet: Small ICBM Hard Mobile Launcher*, available via the Hill AFB website at http://www.hill.af.mil/library/factsheets/factsheet_print.asp?fsID=5717&page=1.

[35] Pat McKenna, *A Taxonomy of Definitions and Types of Instability*, provided for the U.S. Strategic Command, 20 November 2000, unpublished.

[36] GAO, *Nuclear Weapons: DOD and NNSA Need to Better Manage Scope of Future Refurbishments and Risks to Maintaining U.S. Commitments to NATO,* May 2011, GAO-11-387.

[37] Dave Majumdar, *USAF leader confirms manned decision for new bomber*, 23 April 2013, available from the Flight Global website, http://www flightglobal.com/news/articles/usaf-leader-confirms-manned-decision-for-new-bomber-385037/.

[38] *PE 0604932F: LONG RANGE STANDOFF WEAPON*, available from http://www.dtic mil/descriptivesum/Y2013/AirForce/stamped/0604932F_5_PB_2013.pdf.

[39] LT GEN James M. Kowalski, *Status of Air Force Strategic and Nuclear Systems*, Department of the Air Force, Presentation to the Senate Armed Services Committee, Strategic Forces Subcommittee, April 17, 2013, available from the website of the Senate Armed Services Committee, http://www.armed-services.senate.gov/statemnt/2013/04%20April/Kowalski_04-17-13.pdf

[40] Broad Agency Announcement (BAA), *US Air Force Nuclear Weapons Center (AFNWC), Program Development and Integration Directorate (AFNWC/XZ) Ground Based Strategic Deterrence*, 7 January 2013, BAA-AFNWC-XZ-13-001, available from https://www.fbo.gov/?tab=documents&tabmode=form&subtab=core&tabid=2d5eec29c02d7efc3649e8fb e54ecc75.

[41] Ronald O'Rourke, *Navy Ohio Replacement (SSBN[X]) Ballistic Missile Submarine Program: Background and Issues for Congress*, March 14, 2013, Congressional Research Service, doc. no. R41129, available from https://opencrs.com/document/R41129/.

[42] U.S. Dept. of Energy, *Fiscal Year 2014 Stockpile Stewardship and Management Plan, Report to Congress, June 2013*, Washington, DC, available from the website of the National Nuclear Security Administration, http://nnsa.energy.gov/sites/default/files/nnsa/06-13-inlinefiles/FY14SSMP_2.pdf.

[43] NATO, *Strategic Concept for the Defence and Security of the Members of the North Atlantic Treaty Organization, Adopted by Heads of State and Government at the NATO Summit in Lisbon 19-20 November 2010*, available from the NATO website, http://www.nato.int/strategic-concept/pdf/Strat_Concept_web_en.pdf.

[44] Australian Department of Defence, *Defence White Paper 2013*, available from the website of the Australian Department of Defence, http://www.defence.gov.au/whitepaper2013/docs/WP_2013_web.pdf.

[45] RIA Novosti, *Nuclear Arms Reduction Deals to Become Multilateral – Lavrov*, June 22, 2013, available at http://en ria.ru/world/20130622/181811968/Nuclear-Arms-Reduction-Deals-to-Become-Multilateral--Lavrov html.

[46] Shehzad Qazi, *US-Pakistan Relations: Common and Clashing Interests*, World Affairs, May/June 2012, available from the World Affairs website, http://www.worldaffairsjournal.org/article/us-pakistan-relations-common-and-clashing-interests.

[47] Reuters News Service, *US should dump Islamabad, Pakistan diplomat says*, March 19, 2013, available from the Times of India website, http://articles.timesofindia.indiatimes.com/2013-03-19/us/37843363_1_islamabad-pakistani-officials-pakistani-leaders.

[48] Center for Security Studies (CSS), *India-US Relations: Progress Amidst Limited Convergence*, ETH Zurich 1, CSS Analysis in Security Policy, No. 117 • July 2012, available from the CSS website, http://www.css.ethz.ch/publications/pdfs/css_analysen_nr117_e.pdf.

[49] See, for example, Olga Bozheva, *The Son of Satan Will Break through the American Missile-Defense*, *Moskovskiy Komsomolets*, 20 October 2012 (online, at http://mk.ru, in Russian).

[50] Office of the Secretary of Defense, *Annual Report to Congress: Military and Security Developments Involving the People's Republic of China 2013*, available from the Department of Defense website, http://www.defense.gov/pubs/2013_China_Report_FINAL.pdf.

[51] *Warheads*, website of the Commissariat à l'énergie atomique (CEA), http://www.cea fr/le-cea/presentation-generale.

[52] Presented to Parliament by the Secretary of State for Defence and the Secretary of State for Foreign and Commonwealth Affairs by Command of Her Majesty, *The Future of the United Kingdom's Nuclear Deterrent*, December 2006, doc. no. Cm 6994.

[53] Thomas C. Schelling, *The Strategy of Conflict* (Harvard University, Cambridge, MA, 1960, 1980), p. 9.

[54] Keith B. Payne, Testimony to the Energy and Water Development Subcommittee of the U.S. Senate Appropriations Committee, hearings on "Examining the proper size of the nuclear weapons stockpile to maintain a credible U.S. deterrent," July 25, 2012.

[55] Dana J. Johnson, Christopher J. Bowie, and Robert P. Haffa, *Triad, Dyad, Monad? Shaping the U.S. Nuclear Force for the Future*, Mitchell Paper 5, Mitchell Institute for Airpower Studies, December 2009, available from http://www.afa.org/mitchell/reports/MP5_Triad_1209.pdf.

[56] Amy Woolf, *U.S. Strategic Nuclear Forces: Background, Developments, and Issues*, Congressional Research Service, January 14, 2013, doc. no. RL33540, available from http://www.crs.gov.

[57] See *The Nuclear Planning Group*, on the NATO official website, http://www.nato.int/cps/en/natolive/topics_50069.htm.

[58] *US flies B-52s over South Korea amid North rhetoric*, March 19, 2013, online BBC News Asia, http://www.bbc.co.uk/news/world-asia-21840215.

[59] Thom Shanker and Choe Sang-hun, *U.S. Runs Practice Sortie in South Korea*, March, 28 2013, available from *The New York Times* online, http://www nytimes.com/2013/03/29/world/asia/us-begins-stealth-bombing-runs-over-south-korea html.

[60] See *Deterrence Operations Joint Operating Concept*, version 2.0, December 2006, available from http://www.dtic mil/futurejointwarfare/joc.htm.

[61] For a discussion of the funding history of the RRW program, see: Jonathan Medalia, *The Reliable Replacement Warhead Program: Background and Current Developments*, Congressional Research Service, July 27, 2009, doc. no. RL32929, available from http://www.crs.gov.

[62] JASON group led by R. J. Hemley and D. Meiron, *Pit Lifetime*, November 20, 2006, The MITRE Corporation, document no. JSR-06-335.

[63] JASON, *Reliable Replacement Warhead, Executive Summary*, September 7, 2007, The MITRE Corporation, document no. JSR-07-336E.

[64] *Report of the Defense Science Board Task Force on Nuclear Capabilities, Report Summary*, December 2006, Office of the Undersecretary of Defense for Acquisition, Technology, and Logistics, available from http://www.defense.gov/npr/docs/dsb%20nuclear%20capabilities%20foster%20welch.pdf

[65] Nuclear Weapons Complex Assessment Committee, *The United States Nuclear Weapons Program, The Reliable Replacement Warhead*, April 2007, the American Association for the Advancement of Science, available from http://www.aaas.org/news/releases/2007/media/rrw_report_2007.pdf

[66] Committee on the Evaluation of Quantification of Margins and Uncertainties for Assessing and Certifying the Reliability of the Nuclear Stockpile, National Research Council, *Evaluation of Quantification of Margins and Uncertainties for Assessing and Certifying the Reliability of the Nuclear Stockpile*, 2008, National Academies Press, available from http://www nap.edu/catalog/12531.html.

[67] William J. Perry and James R. Schlesinger (chairmen), *America's Strategic Posture, The Final Report of the Congressional Commission on the Strategic Posture of the United States*, 2009, United States Institute of Peace Press, available from http://www.usip.org/programs/initiatives/congressional-commission-the-strategic-posture-the-united-states.

[68] Nuclear Weapons Complex Infrastructure Task Force, Secretary of Energy Advisory Board, *Recommendations for the Nuclear Weapons Complex of the Future*, July 13, 2005, Department of Energy, available from http://www.doeal.gov/SWEIS/DOEDocuments/049%20SEAB%202005.pdf

[69] *Report on the Transformation of the National Nuclear Security Administration Nuclear Weapons Complex*, January 31, 2007, Office of Defense Programs, National Nuclear Security Administration,

Department of Energy, available from
http://nnsa.energy.gov/sites/default/files/nnsa/news/documents/Trans_of_NNSA_WC_2007-31-07.pdf

[70] *Report of the Defense Science Board Task Force on Nuclear Capabilities, Report Summary*, December 2006, p. 39.

[71] Jonathan Medalia, *The Reliable Replacement Warhead Program: Background and Current Developments*, Congressional Research Service, July 27, 2009, p. 11.

[72] JASON, *Reliable Replacement Warhead, Executive Summary*, September 7, 2007, p. 3.

[73] Jonathan Medalia, *Nuclear Warheads: The Reliable Replacement Warhead Program and the Life Extension Program*, Congressional Research Service, updated December 3, 2007, doc. no. RL33748, p. CRS-27, available from http://www.crs.gov.

[74] William J. Perry and James R. Schlesinger (chairmen), *America's Strategic Posture, The Final Report of the Congressional Commission on the Strategic Posture of the United States*, 2009, p. 42.

[75] *The Nuclear Posture Review Report*, April 2010, p. xiv.

[76] U.S. Dept. of Energy, *Fiscal Year 2014 Stockpile Stewardship and Management Plan, Report to Congress, June 2013*, Washington, DC, available from the website of the National Nuclear Security Administration, http://nnsa.energy.gov/sites/default/files/nnsa/06-13-inlinefiles/FY14SSMP_2.pdf.

[77] John R. Harvey, "On the Path to a '3+2 Vision' for U.S. Nuclear Forces," presented to the Peter Huessy Breakfast Seminar Series, 13 June 2013, available through the website for the Air Force Association, http://secure.afa.org/HBS/transcripts/2013/June%2013%20-%20Additional%20Informtion.pdf.

[78] GAO, *Unclassified Summary of GAO's SRAM II/T Classified Report*, enclosure to a GAO memo to Defense Secretary Aspin, 24 February 1992, GAO/NSIAD-92-145R.

[79] President George H.W. Bush, *Address to the Nation on Reducing United States and Soviet Nuclear Weapons*, 27 September 1991, available from the website of the George Bush Presidential Library and Museum, http://bushlibrary.tamu.edu/research/public_papers.php?id=3438&year=1991&month=9.

[80] Statement by Senator Dianne Feinstein, *Hearing to Examine the Proper Size of of the Nuclear Weapons Stockpile to Maintain a Credible U.S. Deterrent*, July 25, 2012, Energy and Water Subcommittee of the Senate Appropriations Committee, webcast available from http://www.appropriations.senate.gov/webcasts.cfm?method=webcasts.view&id=3323b75b-a942-4a04-81cf-9fa0bd297564.

[81] Elbridge Colby, *Defining Strategic Stability: Reconciling Stability and Deterrence*, from *Strategic Stability: Contending Interpretations*, E. A. Colby and M.S. Gerson eds., Strategic Studies Institute and U.S. Army War College Press, Carlisle, PA, February 2013; available from http://www.StrategicStudiesInstitute.army mil.

[82] Helmut Schmidt, *1977 Alastair Buchan Memorial Lecture*, October 28, 1977, available in *Survival*, vol. 20, no. 1, January/February 1978, p. 2.

[83] These doctrinal shifts can be traced through the dropping of Russia's no-first-use pledge in its 1993 Military Doctrine, to then-Minister of Defense Sergey Ivanov's white paper, *Urgent Tasks of the Development of the Russian Federation Armed Forces*, October 2003, obtained from the website of *RIA-Novosti*.

[84] Daryl G. Press, *Alternative Futures and U.S. Nuclear Force Requirements*, from *Concepts & Analysis of Nuclear Strategy, (CANS – Theory Team), Supporting Documents* (May 1, 2011)

[85] Dana J. Johnson, Christopher J. Bowie, and Robert P. Haffa, *Triad, Dyad, Monad? Shaping the U.S. Nuclear Force for the Future*, Mitchell Paper 5, Mitchell Institute for Airpower Studies, December 2009, available from http://www.afa.org/mitchell/reports/MP5_Triad_1209.pdf.

[86] *Report of the President's Commission on Strategic Forces*, chaired by Brent Scowcroft, April 1983.

[87] Yuri Kase, *The Costs and Benefits of Japan's Nuclearization: An Insight into the 1968/70 Internal Report*, The Nonproliferation Review/Summer 2001, p. 55.

[88] Llewelyn Hughes, *Why Japan Will Not Go Nuclear (Yet), International and Domestic Constraints on the Nuclearization of Japan, International Security*, vol. 31, no. 4, p. 67 (Spring 2007).

[89] See, as one example, Michael S. Gerson, "Conventional Deterrence in the Second Nuclear Age," *Parameters*, p. 32, Autumn 2009

[90] Brad Roberts, "Extended Deterrence and Strategic Stability in Northeast Asia," published on the website of the National Institute of Defense Studies, Japan, 9 Aug 2013, http://www.nids.go.jp/english/publication/visiting/index.html

91 Kenneth Waltz, *The Spread of Nuclear Weapons: More May Be Better*, Adelphi Papers, Number 171 (London: International Institute for Strategic Studies, 1981).

92 Jonathan M. Letsinger, *Hypersonic Global Strike Feasibility and Options*, Master's Degree thesis, Air War College, Air University, Montgomery, AL, 15 February 2012.

93 For a new analysis of Conventional Prompt Global Strike options, see: James M. Acton, *Silver Bullet? Asking the Right Questions about Conventional Prompt Global Strike*, Carnegie Endowment for International Peace, Washington, DC, 2013.

94 DARPA, *Engineering Review Board Concludes Review of HTV-2 Second Test Flight*, April 20, 2012, available online at http://www.darpa.mil/NewsEvents/Releases/2012/04/20.aspx.

95 Graham Warwick, *Darpa Refocuses Hypersonics Research on Tactical Missions*, *Aviation Week & Space Technology*, July 8, 2013, available online at http://www.aviationweek.com/Article.aspx?id=/article-xml/AW_07_08_2013_p24-593534.xml&p=1.

96 Jason B. Cutshaw, U.S. Army USASMDC/ARSTRATUS, *Army Successfully Launches Advanced Hypersonic Weapon Demonstrator*, November 23, 2011, available at http://www.army.mil/article/69855; and Department of Defense, *Department of Defense Announces Successful Test of Army Advanced Hypersonic Weapon Concept*, available at http://www.defense.gov/releases/release.aspx?releaseid=14920.

97 Heather Clark, *Labs Technology Launched in First Test Flight of Army's Conventional Advanced Hypersonic Weapon*, *Sandia Lab News*, May 18, 2012, available online at http://www.sandia.gov/LabNews/120518.html.

98 Boeing Defense, Space and Security, *Backgrounder: X-51A WaveRider*, September 2012, available at http://www.boeing.com/assets/pdf/defense-space/military/waverider/docs/X-51A_overview.pdf.

99 Richard Mutzman, et.al., Air Force Research Laboratory, *X-51 Development: A Chief Engineer's Perspective*, 17th AIAA International Space Planes and Hypersonic Systems and Technologies Conference, 13 April 2011, available online at https://www.aiaa.org/uploadedFiles/About-AIAA/Press_Room/Key_Speeches-Reports-and-Presentations/RMutzman_and__JMurphy_X-51_Development_2011.pdf

100 Guy Norris, *High-Speed Strike Weapon to Build on X-51 Flight*, *Aviation Week and Space Technology*, May 20, 2013, available online at ttp://www.aviationweek.com/Article.aspx?id=/article-xml/AW_05_2013_p24-579062.xml.

101 *X-51A WAVERIDER*, May 3, 2013, available online from the official website of the U.S. Air Force, http://www.af mil/information/factsheets/factsheet.asp?fsID=17986.

102 Lockheed-Martin, *JASSM®: The Best Value of Any Air-to-Surface Missile in Its Class*, 2012, available at http://www.lockheedmartin.com/content/dam/lockheed/data/mfc/pc/jassm/mfc-jassm-pc.pdf.

www.ingramcontent.com/pod-product-compliance
Lightning Source LLC
Chambersburg PA
CBHW041528280526
45792CB00004B/1416